POWER
STRATEGIES

HOW TO TRAIN YOUR CHILD

All the top strategies on parenting, social skills, and etiquette that every parent must master!

By discussing just one topic a day, and asking your kids questions on each one, you will be amazed at how much they can learn from such an early age.

Implement each strategy into your daily discussions at the dinner table or in the classroom.

You can work on these strategies in a role-play setting: 'practice makes perfect'

ALL THE TOP STRATEGIES FOR MANNERS, SOCIAL SKILLS AND ETIQUETTE FOR EVERY PARENT TO MASTER!

TABLE OF CONTENTS

POWER KIDS

As a nation, we need to rediscover the manners and social skills that make us stand out as a cultured, developed community. Not just for day to day interaction, but in the highly competitive world of education and work. Competition for admission into school begins at an early age – and one of the focus areas for the best places of learning are social skills. Children who develop these at a young age will stand out and will have the best opportunities – and these opportunities will stand them in good stead as they move through education into the world of work. These skills will develop self-confidence, self-esteem, and self-awareness – building the best person that someone can be.

Skills of etiquette were developed and recognised over 1000 years ago – and are still important today. Treating others with dignity and respect creates a society which functions at a higher level. Someone who understands how to use these skills will stand out as a leader amongst others, with the ability to interact and function in advanced groups. The ability to empathise and understand others cannot be underestimated or undervalued – the best, the most successful have "people skills" – and you can never start too early when it comes to learning.

There is a misconception that good etiquette is snobbish and no longer relevant in modern society – and nothing could be further from the truth. Being able to interact with others using respect and empathy is important and keeping a good standard only requires a few minutes each day. For a skill which leaves an impression, this is a worthwhile investment by any standard!

Whenever we interact, we leave an impression of ourselves, our company, our organisation. You are an ambassador whether that is face to face or in the expanding world of social media. A bad impression can leave an impression for a long time to come – an unpleasant experience sits in the mind and takes much effort to recover.

Verbal and visual impact is long-lasting – and always needs to be maintained. Walking from a school or workplace and letting your professional image slip carries the risk of delivering a mixed message. There is also the issue of the image that is expected by your school, college, or employment, even when outside of hours. There are many examples of a "social media faux pas" which has reverberated into the workplace, sometimes costing people their jobs, promotion, or social standing. If you bring your company or school into disrepute by your behaviour, then there may well be consequences.

Always maintain a good reputation – it is easier to maintain a good one than to try to recover a bad one.

ETIQUETTE – THE RATIONALE

Good manners and etiquette are as important now as they ever were. Indeed, we should aspire for our children to grow into young adults who respect others and are in turn respected by others. The ability to interact with people from all social classes reflects on them, their family, their education, and their employers. Those who show this are the future leaders and positive peer examples. The best method of developing these skills is through direct etiquette teaching, where the expectations can be better explained, and a role model is available. This is certainly not a subject that will be learned on the street or on television!

To develop our children into well-mannered young ladies and gentlemen, they need to understand the reasoning behind the training – they need to see the benefits and have them explained in a way which they can assimilate. The earlier this begins – and the earlier they see this modelled – the smoother the path, the easier the learning process.

It is the sad truth that, in today's world, children and young adults are becoming increasingly more disrespectful, selfish, and reckless. Whilst this may not have anything to do with parenting or how they were brought up, it is an unfortunate side effect of some of the influences of the media nowadays, together with peer pressure or attitudes that children see. With etiquette classes, the sole aim is to avoid these unsavoury characteristics and help our children become well rounded, well respected, and confident young people with a passion for life.

Not only that, but it's important to instil, at a young age, a feeling of self-worth and self-confidence. This will help avoid 'I can't do that,' or 'I wish I could do that' moments that have held so many people back from achieving their full potential. As parents and teachers, we must support our children from an early age, protecting them from anything harmful. This includes influences which will have an impact on their development and

progression. As we know, it is extremely hard to see, from the perspective of a child, why some skills are important as they grow. Having positive role models, excellent boundaries, and positive reinforcement of "the right thing, not always the easy thing" will aid them in their path through life. As they grow older, children will take what they have learned from us as role models, and make use of the very skills we as parents, teachers, adults teach them, in education, employment and life in general; to better themselves and make themselves into the proper ladies and gentlemen that we, as parents, would like them to become..

THE SOCIAL CHILD

Does your child understand how to behave socially?

Social etiquette is just as important as any other form of etiquette. Each phase of growth and development requires new skills – and interaction in the correct manner is one of them. The ability to interact with peers and others is crucial as it aids overall development. A child, new at school, that cannot interact correctly will find each day a challenge – tiring, upsetting, a constant battle where they do not understand the boundaries and expectations. Understanding the different social areas and how to best navigate them will enable a child to thrive and develop.

Children develop differently – at different rates and in diverse ways. They are individuals and must be accepted as such. They will have different stimuli, boredom thresholds, trigger points – but they must also learn to be aware of these so that they can maintain the high standards of etiquette that are expected of them.

The first question must address the understanding of the child – do they understand the settings in which they find themselves? If they do not understand the "rules", then they cannot be expected to understand how to play the game. Ensure that they can differentiate between areas where noise levels require a modified behaviour – libraries vs public transport vs sporting events. It is not simply enough to vary volume of voice to match these, there is also a need to self-recognise the external stimulus putting pressure on them. The scoring of a goal, the victory of a team or individual provokes excitement and a "crowd mentality" where the behaviour of others is infectious. But it may not be correct behaviour and the child must understand that a "herd mentality" is not always the desired method of expressing themselves. Again, the slip of the moment may have implications further down the line...

Seeking out these settings as learning opportunities is invaluable if the child is spoken to beforehand and the behaviours can be identified in advance. If the child knows what is coming – and therefore how to manage behaviour – then there is more chance for a successful learning outcome. Sometimes the stimulus is unexpected and the child may look for guidance (for example in a crowd when jostled or pushed, they may want to revert to a basic, undesirable response, when in fact they need to see and understand what is appropriate).

THE INDEPENDENT CHILD

GOING OUT

Social etiquette is something that all human beings should learn and know as soon as they are able to understand it. It presents a set of rules and guidelines to interact safely and effectively with society in general. As a parent, it is natural to be concerned about your child and how they will interact with the world, especially in relation to travelling. Safety outside the home is an area causing rising concern these days, and it is a subject that requires addressing as soon as possible.

Children may need to travel alone – and it is imperative that they are aware of some guidelines. It is desirable to sit near another family when travelling, and to follow the same route each day. This gives a routine which is constant and therefore departure, arrival and journey length are known elements. Children must also be aware that they should not talk to strangers. Similarly, any "secrets" given to them by strangers are inevitably a danger area that they should disclose to a responsible adult as soon as possible.

Children need to know how to interact with others outside the home – being able to conduct themselves safely and correctly cannot be stressed enough. The outside world can be a dangerous place and children must understand this. As a parent, it is natural to worry – the media supplies a never-ending torrent of shocking stories and children should be aware of these for their own safety.

Being able to conduct themselves safely and effectively in stressful situations may be key to protecting themselves and others.

LETTING GO OF YOUR CHILD - ALLOWING YOUR CHILD TO MATURE

They grow up so fast!

Every parent knows the heartache of realising their baby is no longer their *baby*. I have seen how parents, during the children's delicate, developmental years, almost try keep them 'stunted' in an attempt to retain those early years.

Once a child reaches ten years of age, they should be encouraged to make the transition into an adult, with an adult way of thinking and interacting on a social stage. Attempting to keep them in "child mode" will only hold them back from realising their true potential. Children's' brains require careful nurturing if they are to be able to understand their place in the world.

Encouraging and supporting a child, from the stage of learning to walk right through to learning to drive, will help them develop their own learning skills. A solid support network will aid them in becoming happy, well-rounded individuals.

Positive reinforcement is crucial, as are boundaries and consistency. If a child does not know how someone will react when presented with identical situations, they will struggle to learn correctly or safely. Giving encouragement, role-modelling and correction is important for them to be able to understand how to develop their own self-awareness. From this, they will be able to develop confidence and understand how this translates into a successful relationship with the rest of the world.

LETTING GO OF YOUR CHILD - ALLOWING YOUR CHILD TO GROW INDEPENDENTLY

Although difficult, children need to learn to fail. In the modern world, this is actively avoided, leading children to transition to adults with an expectation that they will always succeed. Failing is an essential learning point, with consequences and a slew of emotions that need to be managed and understood. Children will learn from mistakes without parental intervention.

Do not rush to resolve the problem that your child finds themselves in – they will need to learn how to dissect the issue and discover a solution. If the solution is always given to them, their problem-solving skills will not develop effectively.

It is better to discuss the situation with them – to help them see the "cause and effect" of actions, and to help them uncover the underlying reasons. If they can unpick the issue, they will be better placed to find a solution in the future – helping them to make better choices as they continue into adulthood.

Parents and teachers should be looking at this book daily – it is not a complicated process, nor is it time consuming. A 15-minute discussion or learning opportunity will build to help the transition to an independent child. There is much to learn and much of it will build naturally on their daily experiences. Giving them a place to discuss and explore, to understand, will pay dividends as they develop. There will be times that it is challenging, but this is ideal opportunity to work through an issue, helping them to see the problem and then the solution.

This book is designed to break the transition down into smaller chunks of learning, easy to assimilate and assess. Use it as a prompt for development. Parenting is a skill that can be learned alongside the learning of the child – it will pay dividends for everyone.

SHALL WE START BY SHAKING HANDS AND GREETING EACH OTHER POLITELY FIRST?

- If you are struggling to know how many pumps make a handshake - well it is just two. You can start by saying 'How do you do?'

- Make sure that your hands are clean and dry. If they are sweaty, a quick sweep of the right hand down your side, without your hands being dirty of course, does the trick in most situations. Of course, avoiding such is preferable if there is a tap and soap nearby as soon as you enter the venue.

- The older person will be introduced first: "Dr George, I would like you to meet Helen, Helen is my sister. Helen, this is my doctor and friend, Dr George".

- The female takes precedence over the male in introduction. Start with the woman's name first by introducing them to the man.

- A dignitary or person with importance in their field takes precedence over the lesser of important dignitaries or other persons during introductions.

- Now gather your family members or class together, and role-play a character, using the right hand for handshakes, and any props i.e. books kept or moved to the left hand at the time of introducing.

- Practice a great smile.

- Each handshake should be firm - with no finger crushing!

PREPARING FOR A SPEECH

BASIC ELOCUTION
PART 1

- Parents and teachers, let's prepare our kids for their speech or group interaction for the day. Do these exercises with them. Warming up the mouth muscles helps with speech and pronunciation. Work with each tongue twisting rhyme. Say the words slowly, and with as wide a mouth as possible. Have fun and practice.

- Muscle movement makes our speech smooth and, just like a dancer, our movements will only be graceful if our muscles are flexible and strong.

- It's not very difficult to learn to stretch and exercise your muscles. Here are a few exercises and phrases you can use to take your mouth muscles to the Elocution Gym!

- **PRONOUNCING YOUR VOWELS**

- - a…e…i…o…u…a…e…i…o…u

- - aaaaaa…eeeeee

- - iiiiii…

- - oooooo…

- - uuuuuu…

- - How now brown cow

PREPARING FOR A SPEECH

BASIC ELOCUTION
PART 2

➡ **ELOCUTION EXERCISES**

➡ The rain in Spain falls mainly on the plain

➡ Seth at Sainsbury's sells thick socks

➡ You cuss, I cuss, and we all cuss, for asparagus!

➡ Peter Piper picked a peck of pickled peppers.
A peck of pickled peppers Peter Piper picked.
If Peter Piper picked a peck of pickled peppers,
Where's the peck of pickled peppers Peter Piper picked?

➡ How many cookies could a good cook cook, if a good cook could cook cookies? A good cook could cook as many cookies as a good cook could who could cook good cookies.

➡ Very well, very well, very well...

➡ Supposed to be pistachio,
Supposed to be pistachio,
Supposed to be pistachio.

➡ Chester Cheetah chews a chunk of cheap cheddar cheese.

PREPARING FOR A SPEECH

BASIC ELOCUTION

PART 3

- One smart fellow, he felt smart.
  Two smart fellows, they felt smart.
  Three smart fellows, they felt smart.
  Four smart fellows, they felt smart.
  Five smart fellows, they felt smart.
  Six smart fellows, they felt smart.

- If coloured caterpillars could change their colours constantly could they keep their coloured coat coloured properly?

- A fly and flea flew into a flue,
  said the fly to the flea 'what shall we do?'
  'Let us fly' said the flea
  said the fly 'shall we flee'
  so they flew through a flaw in the flue.

- Sally sells seashells by the seashore. But if Sally sells seashells by the seashore then where are the seashells Sally sells?

- Swan swam over the sea.
  Swim, swan, swim!
  Swan swam back again.
  Well-swum swan!

- What noise annoys an oyster most? A noisy noise annoys an oyster most.

PREPARING FOR A SPEECH

BASIC ELOCUTION
PART 4

- Red lolly, yellow lolly.

- Whether the weather be fine
  or whether the weather be not.
  Whether the weather be cold
  or whether the weather be hot.
  We'll weather the weather
  whether we like it or not.

- If two witches would watch two watches, which witch would watch which watch?

- If practice makes perfect and perfect needs practice,
  I'm perfectly practiced and practically perfect.

- Dick had a dog,
  the dog dug,
  the dog dug deep,
  how deep did Dick's dog dig?

- A sad story about Nobody
  This is a story about four people named Everybody, Somebody, Anybody and Nobody. There was an important job to be done and Everybody was sure that Somebody would do it. Anybody could have done it, but Nobody did it. Somebody got angry about that because it was Everybody's job. Everybody thought Anybody could do it, but Nobody realised that Everybody wouldn't do it. It ended up that Everybody blamed Somebody, when Nobody did, what Anybody could have done.

- Hopefully now your mouth muscles are warmed up and your speech will be a lot clearer to the ear. Well done, great start!

15

REMEMBERING NAMES

- Practice rhyming each name to something, once an introduction has taken place, but only in your head! Don't, whatever you do, 'belt it out'. It could come across as patronising. The idea is to remember a name by doing this exercise with your kids.

- Start by thinking of the name as soon as someone has been introduced to you. You will rhyme the name to remember that person's name: i.e. 'Patrick Fantastic'. This is a fun way to learn names, and the roleplay games are truly hilarious when in action and they are practicing aloud with classmates or family members at the table.

- Teach the kids to do this with respect, as we all know things can get a little 'too fun,' with the kids making light of things – no inappropriate rhymes please.

- By repeating a name when an introduction happens, they will remember things, i.e. "It's nice to meet you, Patrick" (Fantastic).

- Whilst they do the introduction, they can practice the two-pump handshake in the right setting with family and friends.

TRICKY TO FORGET NAMES, HOW TO RECOVER AN AWKWARD SITUATION

- When an introduction has been made, and your child has forgotten a name or names, teach your child what to do:

- They will start by saying "So lovely to see you, have you met my friend Charlotte?" and more often than not, that person will come back with their own name, saying, "So lovely to meet you Charlotte, my name is Gloria."

- By then you will be out of a potentially awkward situation.

- Let the kids roleplay with their classmates and family and friends the best way to get themselves out of such a tricky situation, when it's all a bit much with introducing many names all at once. This is also a great remembering game and mental challenge, to see if their rhyming of name skills work!

- Have fun!

WHEN MEETING AND BEING INTRODUCED TO THE WHOLE SWIMMING OR FOOTBALL TEAM

- This is really light and easy, and this is what to do and practice with your family members and class: i.e. "John, this is my baseball (or football, etc) team. Everyone, this is John, your new coach. One by one, please may you go ahead and introduce yourselves to him."

- Or, they can introduce themselves to John when the time is right. Depending on who it is and who the person of importance is to the group, individually it's really important that they go up to the coach (or person) and meet them in person.

- Teach your child to choose the right time to make their introduction to John. There is no point in butting in while John is clearly in a heavy discussion with another person. They may break up an important conversation if they don't get their timing right. Also, it will come across as rude, and John may form a poor impression of you.

- So, practice roleplay in a situation where introductions, as well as timing to get John's attention, are important. Being at the right time, in the right place and managing their urge to be met, without butting in!

- Be imaginative with names and situations in a chosen group setting, you will be amazed at what your kids produce. Allow imagination to flow.

GET UP AND STAND UP - SHOW MANNERS AND RESPECT

- One of the most important things to do is to show people who are older than us, such as grandparents, teachers and dignitaries, that standing up to meet and greet them is of utmost importance.

- Teach your kids to practice this method to show how polite they are by standing up. It is amazing how much respect that person can gain by giving a good impression to the person walking into the room

- Put your child/kids into a roleplay situation with you by walking through a door. They will need to stand up and greet you by making eye-contact.

- Now it's your turn; allow them the significance of 'how it feels' when they are being respected. This encourages great social skills for when they are in their later years, in a job interview situation, as well as a meeting and greeting each other in other settings.

- Teach them these words: 'manners maketh man' - and these words - 'good manners will take you through valuable doors, which even some of the best education cannot.'

- By finding and using quotes, you are using powerful and memorable tools, which are enhanced through the rehearsal of practical skills as well.

MAKING EYE CONTACT - MAINTAINING RESPECT IN CONVERSATION

- Making eye-contact when someone comes up to you, or if you go up to them to meet them, shows a high regard for the person.

- Practice handshakes and fixating the eyes of the other persons, with no looking away. This is harder than it seems. Most people who are socially interactive find this an easy task. Therefore, it is so important, that from the age of 3 years old, our kids must learn these skills.

- As a parent who has a child with Autism or similar, this makes things harder for the child. There is a strategy you can learn and instruct your child. If they are ever in a situation and they have a person ask to shake their hands, get them to focus on the forehead of the other person, right between the eyes. This will make things less emotional for your child. It's a great strategy for kids with low self-esteem and little confidence.

- Roleplay this situation and discuss with your kids that taking things personally because they didn't make eye contact with the other person, is not as drastic as it looks or sounds. Sometimes the other person does not know how to handle their emotions well, and they must therefore not take a bad handshake or bad greeting personally. It's really about the other person and their own habits, not your child.

- Too often we can take things personally, when, it's how the other person was brought up. Also, unhealthy habits from peer pressure and group environments can have an impact. Teach your child to think 'out of the box' on other people's situations in life. Being thoughtful is key.

- Roleplay a game with family and friends where you need to think of the other persons situation, whilst also making eye contact and staying extra polite. It's all about managing emotions.

PLEASE AND THANK YOU - NO EXCUSES

- Say Please, say Thank You, or you don't get what you want.

- It is amazing how those two magic words will get you so much and get you so far. Discuss this with your kids. Be strict with it. Practice passing the salt and pepper around the table by playing a roleplay game. But remember, we as adults also need to say Please and Thank You to our kids. Show your kids that being a great teacher is of utmost importance.

- Sit in a circle, play 'pass the parcel' with Please and Thank You. This is a fun and interactive game which is a wonderful way to show that giving and receiving with politeness is important.

- Practice lowering the tone of voice and asking with kindness, not in a pressured manner, but always with respect and decency.

YOUR RULES AT HOME

HOW TO BEHAVE FOR ALL OF US

- Sit with your kids, or others, in a classroom setting, or at the dinner table. Today you are going to write a list of fundamental rules for EVERYONE to abide by. Create either a chart, or just a basic list. This list or chart, you are going to pop-up on the fridge, or a wall, and each day you can focus on those things that have been done. Of course, we are all human and not perfect all of the time (discuss that with your kids) and see how many rules can be followed each day, for a happy environment at home.

- Each child can also write their own list of up to 10 rules, which they feel are necessary within the home. This practice allows the child to take control of their responsibilities and to try to master what they have written down. It also gives them a feeling of control. Once you allow your kids to take some control and responsibility for the good deeds they can follow through with, it enhances their self-esteem for positive rewards given by you, for good performance each week. i.e. an ice-cream for younger ones, or a playdate for the older kids.

- Teach and discuss with your kids that great 'teamwork' is of utmost importance.

- You will be amazed at the type of rules each child produces. You will see the priorities within each child's mind and then be able to manage with them, in order, what is most important to you, not just them. Then regroup the 10 important topics they wrote down. Keep it simple, don't force too many rules or they will lose interest. Practice a few a day with not too many grand expectations, which could make for an unpleasant environment. Keep your kids happy, as well as keeping your own sanity in the right perspective.

RESPECT AT HOME BETWEEN PARENTS AND SIBLINGS

- When we are at home, or even in a classroom setting, sometimes the last thing we want to do is respect each other. I get it...we are not perfect, but we must try our best to do so.

- One of the kindest and most polite things to do with our kids is to teach them to say, 'Good morning' and 'Goodnight'. By practicing this, we really are enhancing our social skills within the family home.

- Start by practicing with your kids. A lot of families don't do this. As the child becomes a teenager, they tend to stop doing this. Perhaps they have just become too independent within the home. This we can fix as parents.

- If there is ever a situation which has been tried and tested, and which works, after a full-on heated argument or discussion, sometimes actually just waiting until the next morning is best, once we have all calmed down.

- Most importantly, keeping politeness and niceties with the home environment is important for a loving environment and staying connected.

- If you are knowingly distancing yourself from others, try to at least keep the pleasantries. It makes an ENORMOUS difference and gives room for others to reconnect with you.

- Discuss this with your class or family members. Try make an agreement that with all the effort and teamwork, everyone will make the effort.

SAYING BAD WORDS BEHIND SOMEONE'S BACK

- The most important thing within the home, or at school, is how you make others feel.

- Today, discuss the importance of how it feels if someone were to say their goodbyes to you. You then walk out the door and the two people left behind start having a jolly good gossip about you. How would you feel, especially within the home environment? That person can't go far, as it is their home too.

- Discuss this topic and put the kids in different scenarios.

- Roleplay this out at the table or in a classroom setting.

- Teach your child that gossip, and bullying behaviour, is not appropriate in any situation.

- Instruct your child and discuss with them, that by speaking up and wanting an answer for certain situations is ok. No-one should feel left out or pushed out and that these situations should be addressed in the open.

- By speaking about these matters, it helps no-one to feel left out and 'clears the air' to discuss once everyone has calmed down.

TIDYING UP AFTER THEMSELVES - KEEPING ORGANISED, FOR AN ORGANISED MIND

- There is no doubt that by staying tidy, you can keep your mind organised when bigger things matter.

- As parents or teachers, we often think that tidying up means putting things back into place. But what if your child is working on a Lego project, or school project, and they have been focused on this ALL day. Then you come along and say "right, tidy this all up, it's a complete mess". Imagine your kids did that to you when you were baking a big cake, or building a boat in the back yard, and all your items are scattered?

- If your child is in between a big project, which they have created, tell them to do it perhaps on a sheet, or in the corner of a room on a table, where you know things are out the way and they are desperately trying to finish that project to impress you.

- Organisation is not just about throwing the laundry into the basket, although that is important every-time. You also must discuss with your kids what is allowed and what is not allowed, by keeping within the organisation of the basics at home.

- Projects, and finishing projects, are hugely important to the success of the child. They learn these strategies, especially at home.

- By keeping mindful about your kids' environment, organisation is not just about putting things away, but also by allowing our kids to finish something that is passionate to them.

- Discuss with them your expectations and exceptions.

SHOUTING AND SWEARING AT HOME

- There is never a more prominent place where kids start learning these behaviours, than from their own home environment.

- Today, you as parents are going to find a swear jar. Each time there is a bad word said, in goes a penny. Whoever was the most well behaved by the end of the week, receives all the cash.

- You are going to use positive reinforcement with your older kids or in a classroom setting. You will have 50p, for each day of the week. Think about how much works for you. Whoever swears, pays into the swear jar EVERY TIME. By giving this cash to your kids, it creates positive reinforcement. If only to be taken away, it makes them understand the importance of their behaviour at home. You can also do this with them, too parents, it's actually a fun game, unless there is nastiness at home. This can also constitute money being put into the 'swear and best jar'.

- For the younger kids, 3 years and below, stickers and stars work pretty much every time. Over the years I've learnt that young toddlers rather prefer the sticker stuck on them for good behaviour, rather than on a star chart. There are enough stickers in the world. Don't be stingy by giving them just one a day. Keep showing them that stickers can come all day long for being a good girl or good boy. But of course, let them know that you will take one of their stickers away if they do something naughty again. Believe me, they will want to hold onto ALL their little stickers.

- At home, we practice the 'indoor tone of voice', keeping our voices lower and not shouting and swearing often gets through better to family members and classmates in a much better manner. Practicing this is particularly important to keep a good mood between others.

INTERACTING WITH FAMILY AND FRIENDS, NOT JUST VERBALLY

- Today, what we are going to do, is pull out one of those board games, which has been stuffed in the back of our cupboards for centuries! It is time to learn a new skill and sit with each other, with a nice cup of tea or coffee.

- Bring out the baseball bats and balls, or gran and grandad's old croquet kit. Just by doing this, you can build a lot of good old-fashioned fun without the pressure of finding new and up to date things to do. So many times, we get so caught up on the internet that we forget the importance of social interaction at home. These old board games and outdoor games enhance your child's ball skills and bring on mental challenges which are missing in today's world. Never was it a better time to learn new things with the board games you got last Christmas.

- Hopscotch, do you remember that game? Come on, think back to your youth. Noughts and crosses, Hangman. Show them what you used to do and bring back your inner child with them. You will have a laugh.

- Be mindful of when and how long they are allowed internet time during the day. But remember, educational experiences on the internet are so important these days. 45 mins a day is ok on something educational.

- There are so many things you can think of to do with your kids, like playing charades or preparing a paperchase experience in your garden or park. Come on parents and teachers, bring back the age-old loves which take our kids away from staring at a screen all day. The best games are the ones we used to play as kids and which we learnt from generations before.

- Try keep your kids out of their bedrooms in the day, unless for a nap or for an hour of reading.

27

LISTENING IN ON PRIVATE CONVERSATIONS

- This should be a big discussion.

- Start by discussing the importance of, when a conversation takes place on the phone, unless it's of UTMOST importance, then there should be absolutely NO 'butting in'. This must be a strict rule, especially if you are in the middle of an important call from the office.

- There must be no peeping through the crack holes of the door, and even more so, no listening ears or giggling at the door. Discuss the importance of this, and that when you are finished you will be back. It's very important, as the dignitary on the other end of the line may build a bad impression of you, all because the kids were behaving badly.

- Ask them before the important conversation or meeting, if there is anything they need to know or discuss first. It is also up to us parents and adults to give our kids the opportunity to clear a quick discussion first before that important phone call meeting. If at all they seriously need quietening down, sometimes your only choice is screen time, for the duration of that conversation. There needs to be some sanity given in all situations by not allowing your kids to take over with high pitched noise levels - all within reason of course.

- Another important thing to discuss is opening anyone else's mail. They must learn that they can never do this. It is regarded as a dreadful thing to do, unless asked personally by that person to do so.

- Sneaking into other people's bedrooms, looking in their closets, is also regarded as wrong as we have a lot of personal items in our closets. It's considered very bad manners.

- Discuss these important matters with firm conversation and no shouting.

BORROWING AND RETURNING ITEMS IN THEIR BEST CONDITION

- No doubt we've ALL experienced 'envy eyes' for another person's item.

- The enjoyment of borrowing something which someone else has, must be addressed alongside letting go of that item, which we may have held onto for far too long, hoping that the other person would just 'kind of forget about it'.

- We need to discuss with our kids, that when borrowing, we need to use our kind tones of voice, respect that it is theirs and try to discuss a day of its return.

- The importance of returning that item on that exact day speaks for itself. If by chance you know that is not possible in anyway, then say before the item needs to be returned, and if you need it a bit longer, it must be discussed with the owner.

- Don't just forget about it and pretend it will 'go away'. That person will remember and may not loan it to you again, if not treated respectfully.

- So, have this discussion with your kids or class. Communication between the two people is important to keep up relationships.

- Practice in a roleplay situation, borrowing and loaning. Using 'Please' and 'Thank You', with a kind tone of voice. It will get you far!

BORROWING FROM FRIENDS AND FAMILY

➡ The same rules apply when borrowing something from another person, whether it's a family member, or friend.

➡ Encroaching upon another person's personal items, without asking, is extremely intrusive.

➡ Unless they have offered beforehand and said that you can use it any time, don't just go ahead and use it, whatever it may be.

➡ If the person is not in the room and say it's a pen or pencil, something of little value and you need to use it quickly, tell the person you did and apologise, saying you were in a rush to do so and you hope they do not mind.

➡ Put it back exactly where you found it. Never hold onto the item.

➡ Always get permission a second time.

➡ If by chance you finish the product, tell them you will replace it asap. Then make sure you do it quickly. It's amazing how someone will hold a grudge against you if you don't. Remember, they had feelings attached to that item - perhaps they got it from their deceased grandmother...

'KNOCK KNOCK' - WHO'S THERE?

- We are all living under the same roof as a family, and knocking loudly on doors, or slamming doors in each other's faces, is not good. Not only that, they can get their fingers caught in the doors, which would be a painful experience.

- Toddlers are notorious for this, as well as teens, as we all know. But us as adults, during fury can behave in the same way. We all need to learn to scream into our pillows instead. I know it's not always as easy as it sounds, but not managing moods at home with a lot of banging, not only upsets the neighbours, it also weakens the door handles (that's a very good excuse to say, anyway!).

- We must fight this sudden urge. For toddlers, placing the rubber holders on doors and special door security locks is important.

- Discussions on slamming doors, when everyone is in a calm atmosphere, works much better than doing this when people are heated. So, make sure this seed is planted in your kids' minds when they are in a relaxed mode. By doing this, you will get through to them much better, rather than them pushing you to the point of anger.

- Play 'Knock Knock, who's there?', by practicing knocking on doors quietly and in a polite manner.

COMPLIMENTS

- Discussing compliments with kids is a fundamental self-esteem building experience, not just to the person receiving the compliment, but the person who is also giving it.

- Role-play compliments with your kids.

- Act out different scenarios on the necklace the person is wearing, or even their new hairstyle.

- Try not to giggle if that person is looking odd.

- Sincerity is the key here, and you need to show it.

- Accept a compliment politely and say thank you.

- Discuss how we are going to give at least one compliment to a different person every day. This builds up self-esteem as well as great friendships.

SAYING SORRY AND SENDING A CARD OR LETTER OF APOLOGY

- Parents, teachers, coaches, as we all know, kids can be tactless, bullying, and darn right nasty sometimes. And you know what, so can we as adults. Let's not forget that emotions and angry feelings, or feelings of jealousy don't stop once a child hits the age of 18. By then though, as adults, most of the time we've learned to manage it better.

- Discussing managing emotions in certain situations is important.

- If you suspect your child, or someone from your class, has been nasty to another child, we need to help them to speak up, to speak about their emotions and what exactly happened.

- Today's task is writing a letter of apology in a made-up situation, where the child who was not nice to another child, must write a letter.

- Create a scenario in a roleplay game where they make-up a situation, which could happen in real-life. Let the kids plan this out, then practice drawing a picture, a letter or card of apology to give to the person who then accepts their apology.

TIME MANAGEMENT

- Start by discussing how annoying it is when someone does not turn up on time. How does it make you feel if they are over half an hour late?

- Is this precious time of yours lost? Yes. Of course, it is. There are things we can do to make time management more important for EVERYONE.

- Be prepared. Get your clothes ready the night before. Keep items in the same place where you know you will find them the next day.

- Create a scenario of time management and role play it out or discuss an example.

- Speak about letting the other person know asap if they are going to be late

- It's important to be polite.

- They can quickly do another errand if you are running late. You never know, it may work well for EVERYONE.

- Be on time always if you can. It gives a great impression.

OPENING DOORS - WHY THE CONFUSION?

➡ It is basic and simple manners to open the door for anyone. Both boys and girls, ladies and gentlemen should know how it's done. Yes, it's an 'age old' etiquette move, but it's polite and extremely respectful. It shows a huge impression, which is positive in today's world.

➡ A man/boy should be the one who opens the door for a lady/girl. If the door is super heavy, the man must push it open first, walks through to hold it back for the lady.

➡ Walking into an elevator, the lady goes first. The man will press the buttons and ask which floor to go to. Or the nearest person to the buttons can press them.

➡ A revolving door. A man will go first if it's not continuously moving. A lady will go first if it is continuously moving. The man will use his strength to move the revolving door.

➡ If a lady/girl feels uncomfortable about a man opening doors, it is rude of her to behave that way.

➡ Of course, with heavy packages and people who need help through a door, anyone does it.

➡ A man will be the one who opens a car door for the lady.

➡ Not everyone will understand these rules, so practice being mindful of that.

GIVING GIFTS & RECEIVING GIFTS

➡ Speak about the importance of how giving a gift is showing love, respect, and adoration to the person. Kindness in gift giving is a special thing, plus it builds up a beautiful bond between two people. It's a lovely and thoughtful gesture.

➡ Trying to get the right gift for a person is tricky at times. But if you get it right, it's that much more meaningful and it means that you've really researched what another person would love to receive, especially if you gave them their own personalised birth stone on a necklace, or their favourite animal toy as a gift.

➡ If you ever receive two of the same gifts, it's never a good idea to mention this to the person. Say thank you and keep it, so you can then perhaps give it as a gift to another person. Obviously don't make the mistake of giving it back to the same person.

➡ Discussing and creating thank you cards is important once you have received a gift. Or in this day and age, a lovely email or text message, but preferably a beautifully written card or thank you note is far more meaningful.

➡ Showing sincere gratitude when someone gives us a gift says a lot about the person you are. You can see it in their face. A meaningful and deep thank you, look into the giver's eyes with true sincerity. They went and bought this present for you, taking time out of their day to make you happy.

HOW TO OPEN A GIFT & REMEMBER WHO IT'S FROM!

- First things first, receive a gift with kindness and a smile of genuine gratitude.

- The person who gave you the gift went out of their way to find you that in their precious time.

- Start by saying thank you, then opening the card first. This is the most important thing to do.

- In all anticipation, as excited as you are, read that card slowly, as it may have a lovely message for you inside. Say thank you and acknowledge the message wholeheartedly. This is important.

- Then slowly open the wrapping of your paper around the gift. Do not rip it up.

- Even if that gift is not what you wanted, you must look profoundly grateful for what they did for you.

- Understand that not everyone is going to get a gift perfect for you every time, it's the thought that counts.

- Be appreciative, a lot of unfortunate people in the world don't get a lot of gifts.

- Make sure to write a thank you card.

STAYING AT A FRIEND'S HOUSE, OVERNIGHT OR FOR A FEW DAYS

- First things first – take a gift. Mandatory. It does not need to be expensive, perhaps a beautiful bottle of something? Freshly made biscuits. Chocolates, candles, or something delicious and savoury in lovely wrapping.

- By doing this we show the family or friend our gratitude.

- This also creates an easy transition into the house, and a thoughtful one too.

- You may have one of those duplicate gifts from an earlier birthday party in your bottom drawer. Now is a perfect time to give it away.

- Remember the culture of the family and friend as well. Try not to give anything offensive.

PLEASE, NO GIFTS AT OUR PARTY!

- Respect the hosts wishes. Don't take a gift.

- Do take a card - a special card which is of high quality, to say thank you. You may leave it for them at the entrance, or hallway. Don't give it to them in front of every one, or you may make people feel guilty that they did not bring one, and you have a whole party to get through. Be discreet about it.

- If you or your child has already picked out a present, then make sure to give it to them separately from the party.

- By giving a card, you may also pop a little cash inside. Usually no gifts means that cash may be preferred. If in doubt, don't ask, just do it anyway.

NETIQUETTE = ETIQUETTE ON THE INTERNET

➡ So, your child is so close to harm, yet still so far away, tucked behind a screen, thinking that they are ok! As we all know as adults, this is certainly not the case at all, and this is what we need to have a frank discussion with our kids about.

➡ Speak about the importance of interaction online. What to avoid i.e. bullying others, saying dreadful things thinking they are safe behind the screen to do so.

➡ Avoid any bullying behaviour from others. Perhaps they don't want to speak to him/her online. Teach them that it's ok and to perhaps avoid going onto that particular chat which makes them feel upset. Focus on the friends that matter; arrange a play date instead. Avoid anything negative.

➡ Avoid any junk mail. Always ask if they can download anything, it may have a virus. You don't want your whole internet to crash at home. Speak about the implications of actions and what you click on.

➡ Always use child safety lock.

➡ They must ask first if they can look at something online, and if it's ok to search for it.

THE STRICT RULES OF NETIQUETTE

- First things first. NEVER GIVE OUT YOUR MOBILE/ TELEPHONE NUMBER, HOME ADDRESS OR EMAIL ADDRESS to anyone. This should be a strict discussion with your kids at the dinner table or family or class meeting. Even if the person sounds nice, they could be fooling you with illegal photos or what we call 'cat-fishing', which is highly dangerous - and common in this day and age.

- If they see anything really concerning on the internet, i.e. illicit pictures, or content, they must show you at once. This way you can contact someone necessary to act.

- As much as another person may write nasty things to you online, avoid getting into a bullying scenario where you are doing the same thing.

- Don't bully others or troll them online. You can get penalised and your account taken down.

- NEVER use another person's bank details or even your own parents' details to download anything online without asking first.

- Try to do other important tasks in the house in your spare time.

- Don't ever send photos of yourself to anyone without really finding out who they are first.

- Tell your parents or teachers at once if you receive anything questionable online.

- Discuss this with your kids. This is so important!

THIS IS CYBERBULLYING

- Discuss these points with your kids or class.

- Being mean online, via phone, mobile, email, any form of social media interaction.

- Repetition of threatening messages.

- Making a rumour about someone.

- Posting embarrassing photos of someone.

- Anyone you don't know, threatening you with physical harm, sexual content, or threatening sexual harm to a child.

- Creating a forum to go against someone.

- Content created about you to feel like a target and vulnerable or harassed.

- Check your child's behaviours in case they are acting out. Is there something bad happening online to them? Making them angry, anxious, or depressed?

- Discuss this with them gently, try figure it out.

- Are they the bully?

AVOIDING BEING CYBERBULLIED

➡ Ask your child these questions: Do they know who this person is exactly? What do they look like? Which class are they in?

➡ You are always standing by them, so they must not worry opening up to you.

➡ Understand, they may not tell you as they are feeling insecure, scared, and nervous. It may take time.

➡ Check their phone and history on the internet if you can, ask them to use their phone for an important meeting as yours has gone blank. Make up an excuse - but you must check up on them and see what is happening.

➡ Do they want to avoid the social games they are going to?

➡ Contact Google for anything you see which may be of importance to take down at once.

IS YOUR CHILD BEING CYBERBULLIED?

- Discuss with the kids that this is in no way allowed and to avoid social games or social media interaction for a while.
- Remember the bully wants someone to bully.
- Cut ties with this person online at all costs.
- Make sure to tell you, or a teacher asap what has happened.
- By doing what they did, they were very brave. Support them in this.
- Make sure as a parent, you report this person to the head of the school, so the bully's parents get notice of their child's behaviour.
- If this is a friend of yours and the bully is their child, sometimes it's best to go directly to them. Say, there have been some genuine issues and my child is upset about a situation. Often it will get resolved this way. I mean, who wants to lose you as a loyal friend?

WHEN YOUR CHILD IS THE BULLY

- Are they being the bully, or are they just friends with the bully? Yes, it's a tough one to swallow.

- Explain that being part of a group through peer pressure, is not cool.

- Explain, just because they are behind a screen, it does not mean that you are not hurting someone's feelings.

- If they are part of the CYBERBULLYING crowd, that means that they are also one of the main bullies, just in a different form.

- Will you need to punish your child for such behaviour? I'll leave that up to you to decide...

TEN TOP TIPS ON HOW TO MANAGE A BULLY

PART 1

- Bullying is rife in today's society, and it's also a huge problem in our schools. Every day we turn on the news to hear about another young person who has been the victim of bullying. However, there are some tried and tested methods to combat bullying, and whilst etiquette classes and family coaching would certainly be the first step, here are our tips to help you manage the problem:

- 1. DON'T give in – it's important you teach your child not to give in to bullies, regardless of what they want. Bullies only do what they do because they want to exert power over someone, usually in front of their friends, and if your child gives in, that bully has been reinforced as the 'leader'.

- 2. DON'T fight back – on the opposite side of the scale, you really don't want your kids to acquire a detrimental image by getting into a scuffle with another child. Encourage your child to simply walk away and speak to an adult about what is happening.

- 3. DON'T ignore it – ignoring it and hoping it will go away is not the answer. Again, encourage your child to speak to you or to a teacher; or another adult they feel comfortable talking to.

- 4. DON'T let your child become a target – most kids these days will bully other kids based on physical appearance – weight, skin, clothes, etc., so try to do everything you can to avoid that. Make sure your child eats healthily and is dressed properly – etiquette classes will be able to help tremendously with these aspects.

TEN TOP TIPS ON HOW TO MANAGE A BULLY

PART 2

➡ 5. DO encourage your child to ignore the bully – not to be mistaken for point 3, what you need to do is encourage your child to ignore anything hurtful or nasty that is said to them.

➡ 6. DO encourage your child to adopt good etiquette, to avoid them falling into the trap of fighting back verbally, or worse, physically. Again, etiquette classes will help with this.

➡ 7. DO keep in regular contact with the school, but without becoming too prying or over-protective, especially when it comes to high school.

➡ 8. DO give your child positive encouragement every step of the way – one little piece of positive reinforcement can outweigh 5 pieces of negative reinforcement.

➡ 9. DO always listen - give your kids someone to talk to, make time for them, give them plenty of praise, share your own bullying stories if you have them, but most importantly, always make sure they know and understand that what these bullies are saying is not true, and that they're only doing it to try and gain power to make themselves feel better.

➡ 10. Bullying can be a horrible experience for most kids, and not something that we, as parents, should take lightly. However, with the right positive attitude, positive encouragement from you as parents, will help your kids to manage being bullied.

APPROACHING SOMEONE WITH SPECIAL NEEDS

- Discuss with your kids or class that everyone is different, and that we were not all born in complete perfect circumstances. Some of us were born in less fortunate situations, or accidents happen, and that life is never a 'straight line'. We cannot predict what each will experience in life.

- Staring at anyone who's got special needs is a big 'NO NO'.

- Gossiping to the person next to you about the person with special needs, is also frowned upon in a big way. If you need to discuss anything about your confusion, then do it after and at home.

- Put the kids into a roleplay situation, make them act out being not able to walk, or in a wheel chair, how does it feel when someone is staring at you for your misfortunes?

- Discuss being moral to everyone on the planet and how all our situations can change in the 'blink of an eye'.

HOW DO DISABLED PEOPLE WANT TO FEEL IN SOCIETY?

- Discuss with your kids at the dinner table or classroom that disabled people have feelings too. Even more so in situations where there are gatherings and people tend to stare a lot.

- Disabled people prefer not to be called that. They just want to be referred to as people, which they certainly are, just as much as you and I.

- They want to live their lives in the most normal way possible, with as little harm done or said about them as possible.

- Just because they have a disability, this does not mean that they have little intelligence i.e. look at Stephen Hawking, as an example.

- Play a roleplay game: blindfold the kids and give them a long stick of some sort, clear the room, think about safety. Or plug their ears to try and figure out what the other person is saying. Put them into a scenario for them to see how certain disabilities feel.

BLIND PEOPLE AND THEIR DOGS

▶ Discuss with your class or kids what to do in a scenario where there is a blind person with their beloved dog. The dog is there to protect them and lead the way. They are highly trained dogs who even know when and where to cross a road.

▶ Remember, the person is blind. When entering the room, say hello. When leaving the room, state that you are going out.

▶ You can always offer an arm to the person who is blind, by verbally saying so. Let them reach out for you if they wish to.

▶ Discuss what is around you and if other family members or friends are there, either to the right or left.

▶ Allow the blind person to be as independent as possible.

▶ In no way should you ever touch that person's blind dog. It is only for them to use and must never be distracted by whistles or niceties, unless both the dog and blind person are sitting down.

▶ Always ask first if you can touch the dog, and never offer to feed them.

▶ Play a game blindfolded, walk outdoors, giving instructions to the blindfolded person. You will need to work on distance and objects where things are placed, so as not to bump into them.

WHEELCHAIR USERS

➡ Discuss with your class or family members that having a wheelchair is important to wheelchair users. It is an extension of their body. Without their wheelchair, it may be impossible to have freedom. It is their 'lifeline'.

➡ This is the disabled person's wheelchair, not to be used for sharing or having fun on. They are attached to it, so don't think it's a toy for you to go and have a spin on!

➡ Always go eye-level to speak to someone in a wheelchair.

➡ Never move the wheelchair from where the disabled person left it - how will they find it?

➡ Don't assume a wheelchair is just for disabilities. Elderly people use them too, to get around or be pushed around if old and frail or sick. These chairs have many uses.

➡ The wheelchair user is a person. Teaching our kids that is hugely important.

➡ There is only one terminology to use when describing someone with a disability in a wheelchair. And that is the words "a person who uses a wheelchair".

➡ Using any other upsetting terminology is highly inappropriate. i.e. cripple, vegetable, wheelchair-bound, handicapped. There are just words that you don't use, and we need to help our kids to not be pressured into saying such things, thinking it's a joke.

WHO BROKE IT?

- Yes, it's a parent's worst nightmare, your child breaking an item in their friend's family home, especially if it's expensive.

- Firstly, discuss before they go there that 'playing the fool' is not on, do not run in their home and look after anything that they have been given to play with, with utmost care and attention.

- If something is broken, like a glass or plate, make them say sorry and apologise, going directly to the parents.

- As a parent, unfortunately you will need to offer a replacement or to pay for it. Discuss these matters with your kids before they go to the friend's house. Hopefully, the item broken won't be expensive!

WHAT MAKES SOMEONE A GOOD SPORT?

- These are the strategies to use with your kids and how they can behave to be a good sport!

- Firstly, this is their behaviour on and off the field. How they behave tells a story of who they are and how they manage their emotions, whether they win or lose.

- Discuss that shaking their opponent's hands is important and respectful, with a smile and eye-contact.

- Be a team and work together as one.

- Always show respect when the National Anthem is played.

- Always respect the referee's decision, whether you like it or not. Don't shout or be disrespectful, you may be penalised.

- Always show respect and shake hands at the end of a game, even if you are the losing team.

- If you win, don't 'rub it in'. Practice your 'poker face', with a small smile. No need to make the opposing team feel bad. You can celebrate away from them.

- Remember we will not always be winners, sometimes we lose, and with those mistakes we learn.

- Create a scrapbook with all your sporting mementoes.

VALUABLE TEAMWORK

- Start by discussing what a valued team member is. How should they behave, especially if they are better at this sport than the rest of the team?

- Showing off and speaking about how good they are is not a good look. By keeping modest behaviour, you will gain much respect from the people watching the game and your teammates. Remember, without them, they would not be where they are now. We all work together to improve. Some look up to others with notable talent.

- Always follow the rules, like everyone else. You don't want to be kicked off the team.

- Temper management is incredibly important.

- Always have your own items i.e. water bottle etc on tap.

- Play the game with honesty.

- Don't pass the blame.

- Inform the coach of any issues with team members.

- Look smart, always shower, and hop into a new set of clean clothes after the game.

- Never walk out the locker room smelling badly if you can help it - or get home quickly to smarten and freshen up asap.

- Arranging a team gathering is a great idea, either at a local restaurant or even at your home.

THE IMPORTANCE OF DRESS – CODE

PART 1

- We all know that "First Impressions Count". What we wear and our deportment portrays us as individuals and as a group. People, whether they are adults or kids, are often judged instantly on the way they are dressed.

- Dress Code. Dressing smartly and appropriately can only be a positive way of life, since those judging you will certainly form a higher opinion of you based on your clothes. Encouraging your child to dress in an appropriate way really does contribute to how others perceive your child. If you as a family dress smartly, but your child does not, the first judgement will always sadly be 'what went wrong?' Now, the simple fact is that there may be nothing wrong with your family or your child at all, but those first few milliseconds of judgement based on you and your child's dress codes are all that other members of the public will see.

THE IMPORTANCE OF DRESS – CODE

PART 2

- It is simply not acceptable for anyone to dress and behave inappropriately in public. As human beings, we have a role as the most intelligent, versatile creatures in the world. If we dress or behave inappropriately in public, we are automatically judged, and how highly people think of us will automatically be altered in a negative way.

- Peer pressure and dress code. There are times in a child's life when they are encouraged by their peers, friends or fellow students to dress in the 'trend of the moment', but a parent should try to have a few rules about what should and should not be worn. It's a good idea to emphasize the importance of a good dress code for your child from a young age, and it's equally important to enforce the fact that they simply do not need to dress the same way as their peers. Importantly, what should be instilled in a child is that it is more important to be a good "Role Model" and not follow fellow peers' poor social skills and distasteful dress code because ultimately, it is a good demeanour and positive attitude that will enhance their lives and encourage them to be happy, confident adults.

BASIC HYGIENE & GIVING A GOOD IMPRESSION

- We know how much of a sensitive subject personal hygiene can be. How we discuss it with our kids is a different matter, and often one they don't want to listen to.

- Start by showing them, from an early age, the places most important to wash, rather than having a full on, sit down discussion in later years. They should have learnt this step by step, growing up.

- Discussing appearance is important, and it starts by how clean we are under our garments, rather than the clothes we wear. Smelling good is important, especially having clean hair and extra clean manicured nails. Increasingly, boys/men are taking pride in skin creams, manicures etc. And it's ok in this day and age to do so!

- Make sure you speak about 'dressing for the occasion'. You would not go to a formal wedding in trainers. No, you will go in formal shoes, or a classy dress without looking provocative. If you get an invitation to a fancy-dress party, you must dress up, or look the odd one out. Going 'with the flow' of dress code shows respect to the host.

- Wearing clean, well put together clothes, gives a good impression. You don't need to buy new clothes all the time. Mixing and matching older items with new accessories does the trick. Just make sure to discuss with your kids that clean clothes, which are well ironed, are most important. Some items don't need ironing. Scruffy is not a good look - you won't be taken seriously in an interview. Teach your child this from an early age. It may be ok when younger, but not as we become adults, in the 'real world'.

- Try not to show off with statement clothes. Going 'understated' if you can afford designer clothes, shows dignity and respect in certain situations, with those less fortunate than you are financially. You will be the one feeling out of place if you do that. Modest clothing shows

that you are aware of each gathering you attend. You will figure out what is appropriate or not. It does take practice and skill to choose the right outfit for certain occasions. So, all is forgiven! ;-)

- A wonderful activity to create with the kids. Have them create a scrap book, with what they would consider formal, smart–casual, casual, even scruffy (for comparison) etc. Different dress codes - find as many as you can. Then discuss their options, opinions etc at the end.

PERFUMES AND COLOGNES

- Discuss with your class or kids the potency of perfumes, colognes, and other various smelling additives to your body.

- There is nothing worse than being in a confined space i.e. car, lift, shut room, with a person that has put on way too much perfume or cologne.

- This is how you do it correctly – spray the perfume or cologne about an arm's length away from your chest, then walk into the actual spray. Turn around in the spray so it lands on your clothes, never on naked skin. Your clothes are where it will stick. Only spray ONCE. Done.

- Only spray after your bath or shower. There is nothing more gross than perfume mixed with bad B.O. (body odour). Believe me, people with a keen sense of smell, will smell you and just want to vomit. It does not cover up any smell. It just makes it worse.

- If you are in a situation where you can't get to a shower, just try find the nearest tap, with hand soap and give those armpits a good wash. Dry with a paper towel if you can. It's better than trying to cover up a bad smell with perfume.

- Understand that what you may find a wonderful smell, is not what others are in awe of at all, so, the key is using the perfume or cologne subtly.

- Some people are allergic to certain perfumes, go minimally. It can also constrict their airways in close proximity - if they have asthma, it may bring on an attack. Be mindful, but of course, that is a worst-case scenario.

- A wonderful activity is to practice with the kids, squirting a bottle of water towards your chest, at arm's length, then turning around in the spray. See if you can do this just once. It's not easy when you have a great smelling perfume or cologne. Remember, 'less is more'.

WEARING THE RIGHT AMOUNT OF JEWELLERY

➡ Discuss with your kids that wearing too much jewellery, you could look a little too 'cheap'. There is a fine line. No-one is saying don't do this, it's just a matter of perspective. What do you want people to notice more, you or the jewellery?

➡ As girls/ladies, by wearing just one statement piece, that is the key to looking sophisticated. Try not to bring the pieces too close together i.e. a ring or two with earrings. Or a statement necklace with just a bangle. Perhaps some tiny stud earrings with a statement ring. Only two pieces of jewellery at a time, that is the trick.

➡ As parents and teachers, of course we know that our kids are going to be experimenting. But it's important to show them what looks formal in certain settings, rather than looking like a walking jewellery shop.

➡ The same goes for men/boys. No more than two pieces of jewellery at a time i.e. a watch and wedding ring, or even a leather bracelet and watch. Boys must take off any string bracelets that look tatty and torn, it may be sentimental, but overuse can lead to a build-up of grime etc which starts to smell. Taking those items off before a shower is important.

➡ Make sure your jewellery is always sparky and clean. Invest in some silver cleaning cloths for jewellery or take it regularly to the jewellers if needed. Another hack of mine is to use an old toothbrush, with a little toothpaste and scrub your dirty and grimy jewellery that way with a little warm water. It will come out sparkling!

A GOOD OLD SCRUBBING!

- Discuss with your class or kids, that those words 'a good old scrub' stays true to the word! This should be practiced and done every day. Some say..." Oh it's bad for my skin". Honestly though, if it's bad for your skin, you should at least be washing the important areas down below at least once a day, then showering every second day. And you know what those various 'bits' are! Don't be shy as a teacher or parent to discuss this topic, it's really important.

- A good skin scrub and loofah once a week to get off the dead skin cells and grime from your body.

- A great facial skin routine.

- Hair washed at least every second day, depending on your hair type. There is nothing worse than a stench from a person's head, mixed with sweat, when they have kept oil brands in it for too long. And believe me, others can smell it.

- Cutting and trimming nails. Manicuring your cuticles and clean nails are important things to do.

- Washing hands every time you come into the venue or your home. Before and after dinner. Washing not just your palms, but on top of your hands, around the nails and even your wrists.

- Practice washing hands for no less than 20 seconds, with a good bacterial hand wash or warm water and persistence. It's a proven fact that anything less than that does not do the job properly.

- Practice walking out the front door, making sure you use a hand sanitizer, then walking into the house, after washing hands, using a hand sanitizer again.

- Practice carrying a hand sanitizer around in your pocket or bag and using it before and after going in and out of venues. As we all know, there are viruses around us which are dangerous in today's day and age. Washing hands consistently is the key to staying well and not getting sick.

- Keep those nails clean at all times. The worst impression you can make is having filthy nails. That is one of the first things people look at when they meet you.

THE PITFALLS OF PUBLIC GROOMING PRACTICES

➡ Ok, this needs to stop right now, these are a big NO NO!

➡ Clipping your nails in public i.e. trains, buses, confined spaces with others. You do this, in the bathroom or outside. Never around others. How gross!

➡ Putting your make-up on, on the train, or anywhere visible to others. Practice doing this before you leave the house, or plan to get to the venue earlier i.e. work or a party to do it in time. There is nothing more annoying than to see someone do this in public, pulling faces and spreading their cells around with a dusting of their blusher. Yuk!

➡ Spraying perfume - no, you do this at home first, or at your destination, not in proximity of others. No other option.

➡ Brushing your hair on public transport, where it goes places, or in the kitchen for someone to eventually find it hanging from their mouth, after eating a spoon of soup.

➡ Painting your nails or filing your nails in public places. This is the most gross practice one can do. Not only is there a potent smell from the varnish, your fingernail shavings are flying in the air for others to breath in. Absolutely disgusting.

➡ Step away from the table or gathering to blow one's nose. Then wash hands, asap.

➡ Cough with your hands over your mouth. Then use sanitizer. Or sneeze into the crease of your bent arm.

➡ Always carry tissues if you can.

➡ Any form of grooming should be done privately. No exceptions.

BRUSHING YOUR TEETH AND HAVING FRESH BREATH

- Discuss with your class or kids that having fresh breath and teeth which are not caked in build-up is so important.

- It does not matter how our teeth grow, we are not all perfect and we don't all have perfect teeth. But what is fundamental to everyone is keeping our teeth hygienically clean every step of the way.

- Brush twice a day. Brush your tongue especially, which holds a lot of bacteria. Brush your cheeks gently and all around the skin in your mouth. You will be amazed what comes off. The number of bacteria we hold in our mouths is immense.

- Floss, at least once a day. This takes practice, but it's good practice to do this.

- Use a mouth wash which feels right for you, rinse, and spit. Take in a little water and rinse again.

- Don't brush too hard, as it wears away your gums and enamel.

- Rub just a tiny bit of toothpaste on your teeth again, leave it on for a few minutes, then just give one rinse and spit.

- After eating anything acidic or with sugar, swish water in your mouth immediately afterwards to avoid erosion.

- Have regular cleans every six months with your dentist.

- Eat healthily every day to keep the roots of your teeth healthy and avoid rotting of your teeth. Always stay healthy.

- Avoid sugary foods.

- Remember to brush those molars right at the back of your mouths. And SMILE with your pearly whites!

- Your teeth are one of the things people first notice about you, always keep your teeth clean and your breath smelling odourless and fresh.

- Don't be lazy with your teeth. We only have one set, and once they are gone, there are no more to grow when you become an adult.

- Practice brushing well.

THE RIGHT POSTURE & AVOIDING 'THE SLOUCH'

- Discuss with your class or kids that slouching makes one look unconfident, not really interested, gives you bad posture, and even a hunch-back in the long term. Walking tall and staying tall (even if some of us are short) makes us not only look the part but gives a great impression of confidence.

- Practice with the kids, walking tall and focusing on a point in the room at eye height, not walking with their head down. Show your confidence, it's really important to walk up to someone and give a super handshake, by meeting their eyes from across the room. Try this, and practice daily.

- A fun activity to introduce to your class or at home is to pretend you are a puppet on a string, bend over and touch your toes. Use an example of an imaginary string pulling them up from the top of the spine, behind their necks, lifting them up tall into the sky.

- Once that is done, stand straight up, backs like tall soldiers. No slouching.

- Discuss the importance of standing tall and how bad posture, is not good for anyone in later life. It also gives a bad impression of sloppiness and lack of confidence.

- Especially practice sitting up straight at the dinner table, or your chair at school. Or in the office, mums and dads! Same applies to you! ;-)

USING THE TOILET, BATHROOM AND SINK, AT HOME AND AT A FRIENDS HOUSE

- Firstly. Please may we all try to use the word LOO, rather than toilet when we are in a formal setting. Or saying, "excuse me, I am just going to the Ladies or Gents". Just don't say you are going to the toilet, it sounds crass. Sorry for offending anyone, but now you know. The word 'toilet', well it's just a gross sounding word and no-one really wants to know the exact destination you are heading to.

- If you are in a formal restaurant setting, you would not even mention where you are going, you would just excuse yourself from the table instead, saying you will be back shortly. That is if you are an adult. Of course, we all need to know where our kids are heading when we are out.

- Do hang up your towel after a shower or bath, open, not folded. Dry any water splashes on the floor with a drying cloth.

- Make sure to clean out the sink after EVERY USE. No one wants to see left over saliva or shavings after your use.

- A big NO NO. Boys – please make sure you don't pee on the floor. There is nothing worse than anyone standing in it and traipsing it on the soles of their feet around the house. There is a distinct way for boys to pee at home without making a mess there or at a friend's house. They should just sit down.

- Girls – a big NO NO, don't put sanitary towels down the loo. Most importantly girls/ladies must wrap sanitary towels up well in loo roll and place them in a separate plastic bag. Throw that bag away asap once finished. DO not let it sit there in the bathroom for ages.

- Washing hands after EVERY TIME you have been to the bathroom. (No exceptions).

- Toothpaste marks in the mirror must be cleaned, and taps disinfected, as well as the loo regularly. If any faeces land on the loo seat, it must be wiped off at once with loo roll, or a wiping rag and disinfectant.

- Close the toilet lid EVERY TIME you flush. It's been proven that faeces can fly out metres if not closing the lid. Ewww...yes, it's true!

CHEWING GUM

- Parents, teachers, or anyone discussing a topic as such with their kids. Let's be frank here, chewing gum looks pretty cheap and tacky. If your kids can chew gum, then best give them some ground rules on the subject. If they don't listen, then don't allow them to chew it at all. Really...kids should not chew gum, there is no real reason for it other than having something to do with their teeth. And it's not good for teeth in the long run, as it causes decay.

- Discuss with your class or kids that chewing gum in public places is a big NO NO.

- They must not stick it anywhere when the flavour has run out. Nor must they flush it down the loo. They must place the gum in a tissue when throwing it away in the bin and never into the toilet bowl.

- Never make chewing sounds. It sounds terrible for anyone standing nearby.

- If they have to offer others, then they must do so and share a piece of their pack of gum with others around them.

- Really though, try not to chew gum. Try not to get into the habit unless necessary for personal reasons. Sometimes people will chew gum to stop smoking or for anxiety.

- Don't let everyone hear that you are doing it.

- Always keep your mouth closed when chewing gum, and don't stuff the whole pack into your mouth at once. We all know that bubble-gum tastes delicious with all the unhealthy additives.

- Chewing gum certainly does not give a good impression.

THE ONE WHO'S WEARING BRACES

- Too often we laugh and tease people who are wearing braces. Kids, as we know can be cruel. We as teachers and parents need to stop that immediately.

- Firstly though, instructing our kids about the importance of hygiene wearing these comes first. Anyone wearing braces on their teeth as we know, needs to be super clean and brush their teeth and braces after EVERY meal.

- There is nothing worse than seeing braces caked in food when someone is talking with you. Cleanliness first. No exceptions.

- When taking your braces out of your mouth, do this in private. No-one wants to see strings of saliva whilst you are pulling them out.

- SMILE, it's important you keep up your confidence. Short term visual strain, for long gain. Keep your smile beautiful and happy.

- Stay away from anyone that teases you.

- Try not to put your fingers in your mouth, fiddling with the elastic bands. If you need to do this, go to the bathroom to do so, then wash hands thoroughly.

- As adults, we need to teach our kids that teasing anyone with braces is inappropriate - and they will have better looking teeth than most of us once the dentist removes them.

BLOWING NOSES

➡ There are some people that approve of blowing your nose at the table by moving your head to the side and doing so. What other people may consider is ok to do so, others will not.

➡ If you are out and sitting in a restaurant with a runny nose, make sure to remove yourself from the table to blow your nose.

➡ No-one wants to hear your nose being blown mid meal. A lot of people feel a disgusting feeling in the back of their throats, imagining what may be coming out your nose after each mouthful. Just remove yourself from the table and blow it in the Ladies or Gents.

➡ As a parent or carer, take your child to the bathroom, depending on the formality of your situation. You will be able to judge when it's necessary to remove your child.

➡ Always put the tissues in the bin, then wash your hands. This is another reason it's so important to go to the bathroom. Germs can spread quickly.

➡ Teach your kids never to use a napkin to blow their nose, unless you have paper napkins to walk away from the table with.

➡ NEVER use the back of your hand.

➡ If you or your child has a cold, after EVERY blow, make sure to keep that sanitizer in your bag to use it afterwards.

SAVING OUR ENVIRONMENT - STAYING GREEN!

➡ There is no doubt in our lives right now that 'being green' is the absolute best we can do for all of us. But the hard part is instructing our kids as well as adults who break the rules, that nothing will EVER change unless we all come together to beat climate change for good.

➡ Discuss with your class or kids that by doing the right thing and not just leaving rubbish for others to pick up is important.

➡ Pollution comes in many forms. Discuss all the different forms of pollution, from transport to noise pollution. Gases in the air create toxic waste and we must all know where to put certain wastes within the home. Also, which bins to use. You will have three bins outside your house. Black for general house waste, a green bin for recycling plastic and cardboard and a smaller bin for throwing away just food waste with biodegradable bags.

➡ Do an activity with the kids, gather them all up and grab some bin bags, head out of the house or into the school grounds, and do a litter pickup run. Make sure to all wear gloves. We all need to do this together.

➡ Teach the kids that they could get fined by the police if they just dump litter anywhere or allow it to fly out a car window whilst on the highway.

➡ Keeping our environment clean and tidy is important.

DEVELOP A STRATEGY TO TURN YOUR HOME INTO A 'GREEN HOME

- Discuss with your class or family members that by creating a long term strategy at home to turn it into a planet saving, 'green mean planet saving machine' is key to saving our environment, and doing good on our earth as humans. We ALL need to do this, not just a few of us. Imagine we all did this, no exceptions, wouldn't we feel great and not guilty with just the small straightforward and logical things to do saving our planet? I mean, how many planets do we have to live on?

- So a few strategies to practice within the home are crucial, not only that, it gives us order as well as helping the dustbin men and recycling centres, when they come to pick up our rubbish. Yes, we all need to do our bit. There is a system that everyone should abide by.

- Firstly. Turning off lights at home in each room, as you leave and enter.

- Turn off plugs after use, yes - they use up electricity.

- Eat local produce.

- Reuse the same water bottle. Use your own takeaway coffee mug.

- Discuss how to use the different dustbins outside our houses. We should have figured this out by now...black for general waste, green for recycling (wash out plastics before placing them in the recycling bin) and the small brown one for food. You would have either received recycling biodegradable bags, or you can buy your own for these brown bins. Plus, it's a great way of not letting your black bin sit for too long with smelly foods. Your black bin rubbish bin can sit for a lot longer until it's filled up, I can assure you.

- The little brown bin is the best! It makes life super easy to throw your leftovers in there and dispose of regularly, I can assure you. Plus, it saves on using large black bin bags continuously.

- Reuse any old plastic carry bags for shopping or buy a few tote bags for the kitchen. Don't forget to leave one in your bag, or school backpack.

- Go green, try walking or cycling to school, sharing car journeys, or hopping on the local bus route. You will know when your kids are mature enough to do this as a parent. Only you can judge your own child's abilities.

TEACHING OUR KIDS HOW TO 'SHOP GREEN'

- Yes, we are ALL learning right now, all the new methods which have made us change our ways over the recent years. At least our kids are starting to see this from an early age, thinking it's the 'norm'. The fact is, it's really us adults who've lived through the generations of being the litter bugs of society. Let's face it, not until recent years have we all had to change our habits. Here we are, now trying out hardest to discuss these topics with our kids, feeling frustrated that our lemons are not packed away in plastic, ready for us to just pick up and head home. We now need to wash our unpacked veg, even if it says washed and dried.

- So, let's start discussing what to do, and how we are going to get through all this, until someone invents an incredible biodegradable form of packaging, that no-one has ever thought of before.

- Firstly, carrying our own tote bags to the grocers, is necessary. No exceptions these days, unless you have many old plastic reusable bags.

- Hold onto old containers and even takeaway plastic boxes. Use them for grains, etc if they are loose from the supermarket.

- Buying local saves our environment from the fumes from transport.

- Organic food saves on pesticide use.

- Always buy meals in closer spurts together, rather than stocking up. Often, we won't eat half of the food we buy, which makes us throw a lot away.

- Create a large art project on paper. Categorise it into sections on what is positive and negative for the environment. Half the project is the positive reinforcement of what we can do. The other half is the negative impact of what we do to the environment. Do this project as a team.

- Pop it up on your kitchen or classroom wall.

'GOING GREEN' - BIRTHDAY PARTY

➤ Teachers and parents, let's all face it, not only is this a tough subject but we are starting 'the green birthday party trend'. It's becoming more and more common these days. Most parents are not wanting to spend huge amounts on their kids parties, and actually even with the elitist families, one of the trendiest things to do nowadays, is to 'go green'. It also makes our parties for kids a little more formal than using plastic paper cups and plastic plates. Let's see how we can all come together and make this happen - here are a few tips.

➤ Wrapping paper. By teaching our kids to unwrap the present slowly, keeping the paper nicely folded, as well as the paper bags one can gift you with a present, ribbons etc, these are all things that are marvellous to keep in a 'bottom drawer'. Hold onto all the cards each year, reuse them by ripping off the front picture and then using them as art projects to create cards at home, for any up and coming parties, Christmas and other events.

➤ Purchase some inexpensive and reusable plate sets for yearly parties. If they break, then it's ok. You can find them in a charity shop. A lot of recycled plastic gets remade into plates which can go into the dishwasher, filled with various bright colours. Perhaps buy a set. Have proper washable or reusable tablecloths.

➤ Buy cheaper utensils, which can be used at Christmas and kids parties, year in and year out. This will stop you spending a lot of money each year and creating unnecessary waste. So, keep these sorts of items for the 'party cupboard'.

➤ Use digital for invitations, sent directly to email addresses. Or get the kids to use the old cards to create individual cards for invites, you just need to get creative. It's not always about budget here remember, it's about going green. The budget is a bonus savings measure!

➡ Reuse last year's decorations, no-one is going to remember, unless you have a themed party code. Then pull out the arts and crafts box and start getting imaginative to create the look you want.

➡ Of course, we are not going to be able to use absolutely everything by recycling a new themed party, but we can certainly do as much as we can, to save on waste.

ETIQUETTE AT A FRIEND'S HOUSE - IF THEY DO THINGS DIFFERENTLY

➡ Teachers and parents, we tend to worry about our kids sending the wrong sort of message if our kids head off to a friend's house and say something like, "Oh, we don't do it like that at our house". It's kind of 'cringy' isn't it?

➡ Of course, some are going to be wealthier than others, some families may not bother about the electricity bill at the end of the month and how much we have consumed. But most families honestly do worry and every little counts when it comes to our utility bills.

➡ Teaching your child that each family is unique, when being a guest in a friend's home and how we retaliate, respond or approach a subject is best to just wait and see how things are 'played out' in their new environment, for either their sleepover or weekend away.

➡ Teach your kids that it is not proper to speak out if the host does not do something specific, which you've seen them do or even asked you to do. It's best to just zip our mouths and 'fit in'. There is no point in making people awkward within their own homes when you are with them on such a personal level. It is their home after all.

➡ Boasting about what you do at home, to 'save the planet' each and every time you turn the switches off walking out each room, is inappropriate behaviour and may make people feel they are not doing a good enough job. Plus, you may not get that invite again. Be mindful about how others live and don't comment, unless you are planning on actually living together long term.

➡ Practice this unspoken rule. Perhaps when they come around to your house, they may learn a few lessons

SAVING ON SCHOOL COSTS - FOR PARENTS

➡ Dear parents, finances can be tough for a lot of us. Not only are we thinking of our bills to pay coming in every month, at a rate like no other, we are all also having to think 'outside the box' on how we can purchase items, which are not going to break the bank, after school fees, transport and yearly uniform upgrades. So here are a few things which you can do to save your pennies.

➡ Firstly, use the thrift shop for second-hand uniforms, there is no reason to be buying expensive uniforms when your child is going to rapidly grow out of them anyway. Some parents prefer to spend, and that's fine. No one is judging how you as a family want to bring up your kids, or where you want to put your money. Each to their own, and everyone needs to understand this.

➡ Speak to other parents in the class year above, to discuss possible 'hand me downs' on clothes. Try not to just stick to getting to know the mums and dads in your own child's school year. It helps to 'branch out'. You can make deals with those parents about clothes swaps etc as the kids grow. Or they can tell you when they are heading to the thrift shop and you can buy those items as soon as you get there. Everyone makes an instant deal.

➡ If your kids are old enough and you feel are mature enough to either walk, cycle, or catch local transport to school, then get confident and allow your child's independence to flourish. Or make sure to get some exercise, walking or cycling to school with them.

➡ Use recycled backpacks, paper use on both sides, school scissors, protractors, pens, pencils just need a good sharpening. Make sure to recycle these items every year. Hand me downs are essential. Plenty of charity shops have what you need, or even the pound or dollar shops if necessary, which shops have not been able to get rid of fast enough. You will be spending a lot more at the big chain stores!

- Have good reusable Tupperware for lunch packs. Have a special set of metal utensils the kids must bring home at the end of the day.

- You can go online and find many reusable books etc, plus speaking to the school shops about where you can find second-hand items etc. Your school should already have this in place. If not, it's time for the parents to setup a meeting with the principle.

THE POWER PRINCE

A FINE YOUNG GENTLEMAN

➡ What is a 'gentleman' exactly these days, a lot of us may be asking ourselves. Well, a gentleman is just a well brought up child, who learnt certain strategies from an early age. As well as managing certain emotions within their character, a gentleman does not need to be brought up in extreme wealth. Not at all. You will know if you ever meet a true gentleman. He will have a clear idea on who he is and how to behave in the right situations with respect. He could even be from a poor family but has been brought up well enough to know how to 'hold himself' well in certain gatherings, and with certain individuals. As the saying goes: 'manners maketh man'. Here are some strategies which you can do as parents and teachers to teach our young gentleman how to grow into exactly that.

➡ Most importantly, being respectful and polite. No shouting indoors and asking kindly for things, is key.

➡ Sharing with a soft voice, and kindness. Thinking of others.

➡ Inclusion of new kids at school and into groups. Being an excellent group leader, as such.

➡ Managing voice control. Learning how to debate without getting angry.

➡ Learning great social skills within conversation. Not allowing himself to fall victim to saying something nasty in retaliation. This is a big emotional management skill to learn and can really get you out if a tricky situation, if done right.

➡ Understanding how to open doors, when to 'stand back'. He manages his time with respect for others.

- He offers someone else to go through the door first i.e. a lady or someone who is a dignitary. A gentleman is someone who can also be a dignitary but allows another person to enter a room first. It should just come naturally in his character.

- Teachers and parents, a wonderful way to encourage our boys to do all this, is just to practice at least one of these strategies every day, until it just comes naturally.

- Being a true gentleman will honestly 'open doors' for your child like no other!

THE POWER PRINCE

A NATURAL YOUNG GENTLEMAN

- Parents and teachers, once your kids have evolved into understanding the rules of being a true young gentleman, they should know that mastering this skill should now come naturally. As naturally as saying "please and thank you". You may be guided with some strong points below. No-one is perfect, it will come over time, just make sure to reward good behaviour for them being so well mannered.

- Initiating the very first handshake. Nothing speaks louder than these actions. If he has a sweaty hand, he can quickly wipe it down the side of his trouser leg.

- Opening doors for ladies and important individuals, or anyone older than him. Teachers and dignitaries also.

- Offering to help carry anything that is heavy. Or just immediately standing up to do so, without having to ask. Even better!

- Not swearing. At all. Especially in front of other parents or younger kids.

- Automatically offering a lady to take off her coat. If they prefer you don't, then stop immediately.

- Opening a car door for a lady, or a date. Depending on your child's age. Teens perhaps?

- Always removing a hat indoors, or at the table. Or lifting a hat off one's head when greeting. They can always put it back on again. If their hair is super messy, lift the hat off the head minimally, a quick up - down, just to show respect.

➡ Now get your boys to practice all this, even with you as parents, they should practice greeting you and treating you with the same principles. Don't get angry if they don't do it all the time, these are just young 'gentlemen in training'.

➡ One of the things which is really important, and what will make your boys do well and feel good about themselves, is also dressing well, not looking scruffy, good hygiene and handsome haircuts. Allow them the pride they so deserve. Appearance says a lot, and we all know, the better we look well 'put together', the better we feel. The same goes with kids. I've seen kids' attitudes change in just a moment, when they feel confident.

THE POWER PRINCE

A FINE YOUNG GENTLEMAN'S BIG DATE

➡ Teachers and parents, we all know that our kids absolutely love a playdate. By teaching our little young gentlemen, from a really young age, how to time-keep on a date, amongst many other things, they tend to catch onto the habit of how to present themselves well on a date and court a lady, with much more confidence and self-esteem later on in life. This is where we train them mentally to prepare for when they are in future meetings and so on. First things first,

➡ Time keeping. Arriving for a play date on time is imperative. Not only that, there may be meetings or appointments arranged by parents around these times which are important. Discuss this with your kids and make them understand that it's not just about the playdate which has been arranged, it's also about the importance of the appointments arranged for them.

➡ Prior preparation, at least a week ahead is important. Usually people's week ahead schedules are pretty booked up.

➡ Teach our boys how to ask kindly if someone is available. If they are not, they must try to manage their emotions and ask for a later date, so we know where we all stand with this 'big date day!' Kids really hold onto these days. It's a big thing for them and no one wants to be let down.

➡ Be detailed about location. Make sure you are aware, as parents or carers, if your date has any food allergies or similar. Are they allergic to bees perhaps? Is this a big day full of real responsibilities?

➡ It's really important to exit the playdate without any whining.

➡ Try to always be there 15 minutes early.

- Say thank you for such a lovely day. Even if it did not go as well as you hoped. Just be polite. Smile and leave with grace.

- The boys can talk about any issues when they get home to you as parents. Make sure to plant that 'seed' in their minds.

THE POWER PRINCE

LITTLE GENTLEMAN WEARING TIES AND HATS

- Parents, do practice with your boys how to tie a tie. Give them the task, as well as practicing when and where to wear a tie. Let's start with where it's important NOT to wear a hat:

- During the National Anthem.

- At the dining table. Big NO-NO.

- Never wear a hat inside the restaurant or being seated at the table. Make sure to remove it as you enter the door.

- Indoors at home.

- In the classroom at school.

- During prayers.

- At any formal event where they may be graduating. There are certain hats for graduation.

- Wearing a tie. Where should boys wear a tie? Formal events i.e. weddings, funerals, graduation, meetings, at school if required.

- Boys will soon learn that later in life, ties are worn for many other purposes. Those purposes i.e. interview, office meetings, ceremonies, their own wedding, funerals, and dates, are all important gatherings to where a gentleman must wear a tie. There are many assorted styles of ties.

- As teachers and parents, you can discuss the different types of ties, and practice as an activity where to wear a hat, role-play taking a hat on and off as they enter a room. They can practice tying the perfect tie. Keep it simple at this stage.

➡ Just as an extra activity to do, get the boys polishing their leather shoes. It's just as important to have lovely shining shoes as it is wearing a tie and hat. Dirty shoes say a lot about a person. Allow them to practice tying their laces as well. Untied laces look super scruffy! Do a double bow, so that they don't come undone easily.

DRESS CODE

FOR THE FINE YOUNG GENTLEMAN
MORNING-SUIT

- Parents and teachers, in today's day and age, one of the most important aspects of a gentleman, in mostly any given situation, is his appearance. Not only that, understanding the appropriate dress code, and actually knowing what that dress code means, is a great start from a young age. Understanding dress codes can start from an early age, from teens into adulthood with the understanding of what to wear, when and how to wear it.

- MORNING SUIT – The male figure in your family will wear this suit, suited as wedding attire. There are two types of MORNING SUIT:

- A combination of, dark grey or black trousers. White shirt, grey waist coat, black or dark grey top hat. Lace-up leather shoes, preferably black. Gloves, yellow in England, grey in France.

- Both combined outfits worn with a cravat or tie.

- Which is a combination of grey trousers, grey tails, white shirt, grey waistcoat, grey top hat, lace up black leather shoes. Grey gloves, optional.

- A tie is worn with a stiff, turned down collar, and the pin (cravat) with a wing collar.

- English and French tails are both different. The French is much more fitted to the front of the body.

- A buff is also accepted.

- The gloves must be a soft, yellow colour.

89

DRESS CODE

FOR THE FINE YOUNG GENTLEMAN
BLACK TIE

- We tend to find that black tie for the male figure, fits into many formal events. In France, black tie is pronounced 'cravate noire'.

- Wearing black tie consists of:

- A dinner jacket (wool), with satin lining.

- Matching black trousers (tapered) with single braid down the seam of the outer trouser leg.

- Beltless, with braces.

- White crisp button up shirt, with a pleat down the front, turn down collar.

- Black bow tie (faille or barathea).

- Cummerbund or waistcoat, suited to colour, or even matched with partners outfit.

- Long, black, quality socks

- Leather lace up shoes, patent or not.

DRESS CODE

FOR THE FINE YOUNG GENTLEMAN
WHITE TIE

- It is not common these days for males to go places wearing 'white tie'. This type of suit is for extremely formal occasions. Unless you have been invited to such an event, there is often no reason to really own one of these suits. On the other hand, if you were invited to such an extremely formal setting, hiring a suite for a white tie event would be advisable. There is no reason to go out and buy one for your young child or teen, if they are only going to grow out of it. Then again, if you have extra income which is of no real issue, no-one is stopping you from spending your hard earned cash on a suit your kids may only ever wear once or twice, depending on how many formal invites you have in one year.

- 'WHITE TIE' Evening dress, or in French 'Tenue de soiree' or 'habit'.

- Wear a pocket watch, not a watch.

- Black trousers, with double braid down outer seam.

- Black evening tailcoat.

- Stiff fronted shirt, with detachable wing collar.

- Collar fastened with gold studs, or mother of pearl.

- Cufflinks.

- White pique bow tie.

- White pique waistcoat.

- Black patent lace up shoes.

- "SPENCER"- Which is another form of dress code apart from white tie, this consists of: A short dress jacket without any tails. This can be worn with uniform dress but is not really worn so much these days.

DRESS CODE

THE FINE YOUNG GENTLEMAN
LOUNGE SUIT OR INFORMAL

- **LOUNGE SUIT** or **INFORMAL** outfits, males tend to wear these, especially when they are younger, they tend to get away at formal events wearing this outfit.

- Sober tie.

- Dark navy-blue suit, black or dark grey.

- Smart black leather lace up shoes.

- Fine coloured socks. Males tend to wear increasingly fancy and colourful socks these days, which can 'jazz up' the outfit for different social settings.

- This can be worn to a formal party, or dinner party.

DRESS CODE

FOR THE FINE YOUNG GENTLEMAN
SPORTS AND WEEKEND WEAR, LEISURE, CASUAL AND COUNTRY CLOTHES

- Parents, mostly, you will find your young boys wearing more of these outfits growing into adulthood. When 'put together well', with great combinations of colour, your child can learn the importance of colour combination, with even the simplest of outfits.

SPORTS & WEEKEND WEAR

- Sports jacket.

- Elegant trousers (flannel).

- Brown leather lace up shoes, loafers, or brogues.

LEISURE OR CASUAL

- Smart and simple shirt and trousers.

- For BBQs and Picnics, short sleeved shirt, and shorts.

COUNTRY CLOTHES

- Tweed jacket in the colours of the countryside i.e. browns, greens, etc.

- Light sweaters.

- Coloured shirts.

- Corduroy or flannel trousers.

- Easy wearing shoes, smart trainers(kids) or boots.

- Waterproof jacket, Barbour.

- Hat, gloves, scarf, depending on the weather.

- Coat, Loden, depending on setting and the weather.

DRESS CODE

FOR THE FINE YOUNG GENTLEMAN
A RE-CAP ON HATS, GLOVES & JEWELLERY

➡ Hats to always be taken off in a place of worship i.e. Church, funeral, in a diplomatic setting, raising, or lowering of the flag.

➡ Hats must be removed when entering a restaurant, any closed-in-area such as cinema, cafeteria, theatre, plane, train, car, lift, living-room, living-quarters, shop, or office.

➡ To come across as polite, take your hat off with the left hand to shake with the right hand, when greeting, or you will come across as impolite.

➡ A young gentleman takes off his hat when meeting a lady or superior individual.

➡ In America, a gentleman can touch lightly the rim of his hat, indicating that he is being respectful. He does not need to take off his hat when greeting, although in some other countries, he MUST do so.

JEWELLERY

➡ The basic jewellery for the true gentleman is:

➡ Cufflinks

➡ A "fob watch" watch which has a chain for the pocket.

➡ A "turnip watch" this is for evening dress, a pocket watch with no chain.

94

BUTTER KNIVES & WEAPONS

➡ Parents, this is a big subject, discuss with your kids that using utensils as weapons is a big NO NO in your house. Dads, this is a great subject you can work on with your kids. The best person to discuss this subject with your kids, is the person who you feel has the most influence with a certain character of child within your family. Some kids will listen more to one parent over the other, whether it be an uncle, aunt, grandparent, or friend. This is a tricky subject and coming across in a firm manner about not using utensils, kitchen knives or any cutlery, even as a joke, pointing it others, is definitely a big NO.

➡ As we know, crime has gotten worse over the years, and sadly more and more kids are using their home kitchen knives on each other, taking evil onto our streets. We need to stop this right away. If you have a special cupboard to lock away your knives at home, then you should. Depending on your circumstances, you will know if you need to or not.

➡ As for butter knives and various other utensils, toddlers must know from as young as possible that using them on other kids or siblings to hurt them, is a big NO. Have an in-depth discussion why they should not behave that way. If they don't listen, then it is up to the parents to deal with the situation so that they don't re-enact this at school and put other kids in harm's way.

➡ I think all of us as parents need to take the initiative to fix this problem at once, if there is any danger to others.

➡ This is a 'hard talk' discussion. Without showing violence, use a soft tone. The person discussing this matter must be a major influence on the child.

- Your kids should practice your local area police emergency number, and the number for the local fire brigade and ambulance.

- Your child must know their full names and their parents' full names as soon as possible in their young lives. 3 years old is a suitable time to start practicing, or even younger if your child's learning maturity allows them to learn this quickly.

- Your child must practice their home address, at least once or twice a week as young as possible in case they get lost at the beach or in a shopping mall.

THE POWER PRINCESS

A FINE YOUNG LADY

➡ I see too many parents these days with such grand expectations for their little girls, when they have not even had the basic of general life experiences. We must try not to push our girls into something they don't want to do or be someone they are not. They will only become resentful. As we all know, not all little girls want to dress-up in sparkly clothes, flying fairy wands around the garden. When I was a little girl, I was a complete 'tom-boy'. I absolutely loved going fishing on the dam with my little 'lollipop' boat at the bottom of the garden, and building forts was my thing. I just loved it. Presenting me with Barbie dolls for a birthday present was totally wasted on me. As I grew up, my parents knew that I was never going to be the 'typical little girl' who loved to wear princess dresses, but they still moulded me into what being lady was about. As parents, even if we don't know where our girls are really heading, take the time to still teach them the basics. There are more intense courses on etiquette which a lot of parents would love to send their girls on. But it's not totally necessary if you know the basics of what to do and allow your little girl to flourish into the person she was born to be. There are absolutely no set rules. What I do suggest is that your girls learn the art of awareness. This is important and every girl, lady, mum, grandmother and the male figures in their lives especially, know that if a woman behaves or dresses in a certain way, they will get frowned upon. True to the word, and especially, females do tend to get 'the harder end of the stick' when it comes to first impressions. Being mindful of your appearance in general settings, is key to how you will be treated and how you present yourself. Every little helps, if you understand how to raise your girls for these moments, as people are naturally judgemental. Cultural differences also play a big part in how we are perceived as the fairer sex. Being mindful of dress code in

every situation is imperative. Each little girl is different, you can take what you want from the pages ahead. Only you as parents, or teacher, know your child best and what to encourage her to become, without forcing any situation. We are all individuals with independent minds, at the end of the day. That is, we were all born to be, a 'POWER PRINCESS'.

THE MESSY PRINCESS

PART ONE

➡ Parents and teachers, especially parents. Let's get right to the point here, how many toys are you actually buying for your kids? The key is in buying the right gifts for your child's interest. And for you to be just as organised in throwing anything away (silently, when they are not aware of what won't be missed) if they have grown out of it. That is the first strategy.

➡ Secondly, if your girls are messy, we need to teach them about organisation, and how organisation within their own bedroom, or playroom, also creates an organized mind. So – organized environment = organized mind. For everyone.

➡ Start by discussing where things go. Each game etc has a 'home'. Just as we have a home, so do your toys. Ask them if they would feel sad if they did not have a home to live in - most of the kids will say, 'yes'. If they start playing 'mind games' with you, as often they will, try override their silliness, as the seed hopefully would have been planted anyway. Then keep showing them every day, until they are listening and have got the picture. Some kids, as we know, have behaviours which won't resonate with what you are saying, so 'positive reinforcement' is key.

➡ By asking them every day what they plan to play with in the playroom or bedroom, you help them to prioritise. This way they will usually take out one thing at a time. Try teaching them to put away toys or games once finished. Importantly, if they are proud of a puzzle they have created or artwork etc, allow them to keep it out for the day for everyone to see and admire. Try not to get too harsh. We should all be proud of our achievements. You have to allow flexibility within their 'creative zone. That is where they grow from learning.

99

➡ Take a morning, or afternoon, out of your time, to show the child where things go. Show them the labels. Even a toddler will learn from the visual letters with what goes where. Start training them into doing these daily routines, putting away habits from day dot! Allow them and help them to carry it to the drawer or box it 'goes to sleep in'. It is the toys' home, after all.

THE MESSY PRINCESS

PART TWO

- Clothes for the seasons. Do this task with your girls. Every season pop away all her Summer clothes if it's going into Summer and pop away all her Winter clothes if it's going into Summer. There is less confusion between seasons, even if you have Autumn and Spring to get through. You can also do this with your little princes. They should learn from an early age how organisation in our cupboards not only gives us more room inside them, but also helps us to find our clothes easier for the correct season. Most parents know how to organise clothing as such. Of course, it's great that kids have freedom and independence when choosing their daily wardrobe, but wearing shorts on the coldest day of the year?

- Even helping with folding and arranging formal or casual dresses into sections in the cupboard, has uses. Folding clothes is especially a great task for kids to learn the basics of house management. Everything starts from home and we have to show our kids how to do it rather than thinking that they are a pain to have around when you are trying to do it. Remember, they learn from you, so you need to show them how to do it, for your own long-term sanity.

HOW TO SIT LIKE A PRINCESS - 'THE DUCHESS SLANT'

- Parents, as mentioned previously, our girls are not all equal. Not all our girls are going to want to sit in the most uncomfortable sitting posture either from such an early age

- 'The Duchess slant'. I mean – really - who thought of this sitting pattern? It's not only uncomfortable, it's just not compatible either for every 'Power Princess' in town. But one thing we know for sure, it looks beautifully elegant. If your child is not interested in sitting and practicing day in and day out to sit this way, that's no problem at all. They are kids after all and there is no 'rule book' forcing anyone to do anything they don't want to do. Of course, girls, teens, young ladies - flinging their legs open in all sort of settings is hugely frowned upon and makes them look cheap. No-one wants to see panties flashing across the room. Always shocking if you see anything as awkward and unbecoming.

- So, let's start by keeping things simple. You don't have to slant your legs. Which little girl is going to remember to do this absolutely every day? Although they must always learn to keep knees and ankles together as much as possible.

- Little girls must learn early to sit correctly, even on the sofa where it's comfortable enough to sprawl themselves out. There is a time and place.

- As for the 'Duchess slant', this is how to do it, which you as mums or teachers can practice at home first, before you show off your elegance to the world.

- Never run to the chair, walk elegantly towards it. Walking upright, looking ahead gracefully.

- Calf against the seat or chair as you gracefully turn. Sit slowly, to bring you to a seated position. Back straight. Head up.

- Extend arms towards knees, bring hands slowly onto your lap, place elegantly on your lap.

- Cross ankles gracefully and knees together always.

- Keep hands relaxed and one on top of the other, to the side. When standing up, use thighs, rather than using your arms to lift your weight.

- Go online and look up 'the Duchess slant' tutorials. Your girls can practice from photos and what they see from Royalty.

THE POWER PRINCESS

HOW TO HOST
PART ONE

- Discuss with your kids what a great host is, and how to be one. Some of the greatest strategies to learn and teach your own kids, is how being a great host shows others how welcome they are in your home. By shadowing you as parents, from an early age and not being told to just 'get out the kitchen', is important for them to understand how to host guests. As parents, you really should ask your kids to do tasks when the guests have arrived, from carrying plates to offering tea or coffee etc upon arrival. This will help their performance later in life and help them to grow comfortable with inviting their own guests one day to their dinner parties. You don't have to ask them to do everything, just a few errands here and there.

- Using the time with them to show them how to do preparation of the cooking, also is a wonderful way for them to learn. Here are some tips which your girls can learn. By all means, this is not just left for the ladies to do these days, so make sure your boys are learning too - or they will just expect that their future wives are the only ones who should be doing all this in the future. If they don't want to do it, then make an agreement with them that they will be the ones tidying up.

- They must learn to not just host their own friends, but also the guests of their parents.

- Be as well-mannered as possible with guests.

- Always have good timekeeping, and keep guests informed of any changes as early on as possible.

- Always dress with complete respect to the occasion and culture.

- Always support anyone looking or feeling 'left out' at the party.

- Always use a kind voice.

THE POWER PRINCESS

HOW TO HOST
PART TWO

- Encourage interaction with the whole group, as one unit.

- Make everyone feel welcome.

- Ask if anyone has any allergies to food a few days before the event. Discuss with your kids what certain allergies are, and what can happen i.e. nuts.

- Make it a joyous occasion as much as possible.

- Volunteer as much as possible within the community.

- Always offer to help hosting an event, if a friend or event needs assistance of your incredible talents with preparation.

- Preparing the venue with elegance and style. A beautiful or fun looking table always brings everyone together.

- Focus on the detail and be well prepared.

THE POWER PRINCESS

HOW TO DECLINE A DATE

- Parents, we all worry about our girls, especially when they hit teenage years and are being asked on dates. By starting early on with how they should approach matters is another story all together - one which they must learn to do gracefully and not tactlessly. Here are some strong points to sit down with your girls, and in fact boys (so that they also know the other gender's perspective) on the correct behaviour. Let us start with how your girl, from an early age, should learn how to decline a date. Teaching them young gives them great practice as they get older.

- Without being nasty, or with no 'catty' tone, if they don't really like a friend and are finding any excuse 'under the sun' to get out of an invite, they should state that they have already made other plans and sorry, but this time it's just not possible. If the other person keeps on persisting as well as insisting, then your girls can politely say 'look, I'm really sorry, but I prefer we go our separate ways.' Some relationships are just not compatible, and we all know it very well. For them to decide who they want to spend time with early on, shows real strength. They must practice doing this though, in the most graceful way. It is hard to swallow, yes. The best time to include a person who keeps on persisting on their time, is when there is a large group of kids and no-one has to feel left out.

- Boasting and gossiping about her 'let-down' to other friends, is a big NO NO. She must gracefully avoid the subject with anyone. Unless she is getting harassed, then she must go directly to you or a teacher to sort this matter out as soon as possible.

THE POWER PRINCESS

HOW TO DRESS
PART ONE

- Dress code, parents! It's really just that. Dress code and the protocol to fit in. Each little girl is unique. There is no 'rule book' saying that the fashion police are on alert if your girls do not dress a certain way. Yes, you may get the 'gaggling mums' in one corner of the birthday party, comparing their latest purchases from Harrods with the latest Prada princess dress, which they proudly bought the other day. Most of the time, there are more 'grounded' and less pretentious parents, who are not so hideously 'nouveau riche' about the subject and know very well, that once this party is over, their kids won't want to wear the same frock again anyway. And so, they will also grow out of it. So, to those parents, I'm totally with you. There is no need to buy the latest and most expensive clothes for your kids. If they look, clean, tidy, well washed, and groomed hair, with exceptional manners, then that goes further than designer outfits.

- Then again, each to their own, and if parents want to spend money on clothes which are going to be grown out of by their kids in seconds, that's ok. We are all walking on different paths in life and we should judge less and accept that. But most importantly, we must all practice protocol, grace, and awareness of our gatherings, and making the most of what we've got without boasting or distastefully showing off.

- What makes a 'POWER PRINCESS' dress so powerfully? Here are some strong points below to instruct your girls about looking stylish and sophisticated, mapped out for girls.

THE POWER PRINCESS

HOW TO DRESS
PART TWO

- Hygiene first. Regularly washed hair, at least every second day. Brushed teeth and clean, short cut nails.

- Matching socks or tights with her outfit.

- Try to never use more than two-three colour schemes for matching outfits.

- Accessories which match the outfit.

- No more than two matching hair clips at a time.

- Brushed hair always.

- Coats always looking clean.

- Clothes not too small for them and not too tight. Kids need elasticated movement to play.

- Hats and scarves which match the outfit. Simple colours which will go with every outfit. if parents are the fussy type. If your child likes bright colours, then no problem at all. They are creative and allow them to be that way.

- As parents, we all want our kids to 'Stand out from the crowd' with their personalities and talents, which they most probably always will do. But how about actually 'fitting in'? It shows no truer class, regardless of your background, if you understand this important tip. What came first, the chicken or the egg? Who knows, but one thing that is true to the word, first impressions are most important, along with a great smile. When it falls to appearance and how people perceive you, by working on that first impression, it goes far.

➡ Show them a colour wheel and discuss which colours go well together. You will be amazed when they start to experiment mixing and matching their outfits with their newly developed skill. Need I say no more.

DRESS CODE

THE FINE YOUNG LADY
MORNING SUIT, BLACK TIE OR WHITE TIE

MORNING SUIT
- Knee length dress, or silk suit.
- Hat and gloves, depending on the event i.e. wedding and the country you are attending the event.

BLACK TIE
- Decide the proper attire for the country, religion, and culture where the event is taking place. Which venue is it being held at?
- Elegant knee length dress, if taking place at home with less than 10 guests.
- Formal reception. 20 guests or more. Elegant full-length dress.
- Formal dinner, elegant full-length dress.
- A ball. A full-length dress. Even at an official event.
- A birthday party etc, a full-length dress which goes to the calf.

WHITE TIE
- Long formal evening dress, traditionally open neck.
- Long gloves, mostly older ladies will enjoy wearing these, but not expected of younger generations.
- Materials will be of expensive quality i.e. brocade, silk, velvet, lace.
- A watch is not worn with the above dress code
- Do not wear too much jewellery, two pieces, with one 'statement' piece, is enough to bring elegance to any outfit.

DRESS CODE

THE FINE YOUNG LADY
LOUNGE SUIT OR INFORMAL WEAR, SPORTS AND COUNTRY CLOTHES

➡ Depending on the location and venue, here is the best formal, informal and weekend wear guided outfits, with which any young lady can start experimenting.

LOUNGE SUIT OR INFORMAL

➡ An evening trouser suit.

➡ An elegant dress, skirt, or suit. Dependant on the event and weather.

SPORTS, WEEKEND WEAR

➡ Smart/casual trouser suit.

➡ Smart/casual dress.

LEISURE OR CASUAL

➡ A simple dress, which is not provocative.

➡ Simple tops, which are not provocative.

➡ Long shorts and knee length skirts, for picnics and BBQ's (It is important that young ladies wear suitable undergarments with skirts if going for a picnic or lounging on the grass).

➡ Tight, easy to wear thigh pants, to slim line the body is important, for every occasion. Even if by mistake your dress blows-up in the wind, thigh pants will also give you a better streamline look as well as a sense of security from the wind and the 'fashion police', which as we are all aware, are always 'out in force'.

COUNTRY CLOTHES

- Walking boots, ankle boots, shoes, wellies depending on the weather, flat shoes for indoors.

- Smart/casual trouser, light, or heavy sweaters, jeans are fine, Loden coat.

DRESS CODE

THE FINE YOUNG LADY
SHOES AND HANDBAGS

- Bags should be chosen to suit the colour of the dress and the style. If it's a formal setting, you match a formal bag. There are beautiful bags out there which are not expensive for a one-off occasion.

- Shoes, belts, and gloves should all be of the same colour as the handbag, or well-matched.

- Nude coloured shoes are a good purchase to mix and match.

- Shoes must match the dress or trousers.

- Shoes and handbags can be of a different colour to the outfit. Make sure the colours go well together in contrast.

IMPORTANT POINTS

- A lady will not be required to move her shoes for a party.

- A lady can be expected to remove her shoes at a sit-down meal, perhaps where she is at an event where she is eating lower to the ground i.e. an Asian banquet.

- Dinner dresses are formal. The dinner will last longer than a luncheon. Dinner is served in the evening.

- Be careful not to mix up patterns and prints by the dozen. One elegant and prominent pattern speaks loud and clear enough.

- A tea party is elegant but informal.

- A cocktail dress is a dress which you can jazz up with accessories, then proceed onto a formal theatre production and a dinner date.

DRESS CODE

THE FINE YOUNG LADY
HATS & GLOVES

- When should hats and gloves be worn?
- Hats are never worn in the evening. The cut off time to wear a hat is 6 pm.
- The hat must match the outfit's colours. So must the gloves.
- Hats are to be worn at church ceremonies, funerals, mass, christenings, first communions and weddings.
- Opening of parliament in countries who hold a monarchy.
- Garden parties which are formal events in the daytime
- Horse racing events i.e. Ascot.

IMPORTANT POINTS

- Appropriate dress code must be flexible to:
- The time of day which the event is taking place.
- The country and its religious dress code.
- The reason for the event i.e. wedding or Baptism.
- The climate and the season.
- The local city, town, village.
- Where you are planning on staying i.e. five-star hotel, friend's house or B&B.
- Always pack a long length silk or cotton, easy to roll up dressing gown and foldable slippers.
- Check with the hotel the amenities i.e. blow-dryer etc so you can pack light and not weigh down your luggage

DRESS CODE

THE FINE YOUNG LADY
JEWELLERY

- When and where to wear the appropriate jewellery is of utmost importance. Not only so you don't look like a Christmas tree gone wrong, but also so you are aware of your surroundings, when and when not to wear it.

- Wear jewellery discreetly.

- Jewellery is never worn at a funeral, other than weddings bands or a pearl necklace.

- You can wear more jewellery in the evening. Little during the day or morning. Earrings and a couple of rings in daytime, with perhaps a delicate chain around the neck in the day, is sufficient and elegant.

- For sporting events, merely a small set of ear studs is enough, if you are playing sport.

- For BBQ's and picnics, wear as little as possible, no more than three items i.e. a ring, bracelet, and earrings, all managed with elegance to suit the outfit.

- One statement piece if you are wearing a large piece of costume jewellery in the daytime.

- You can wear both fake and real gold and silver together. Silver and gold together look elegant if you match it well.

- Wearing ankle chains, nose chains, waist chains, do not reflect sophistication in Europe or America. It comes across as tacky.

- In India wearing nose rings and nose chains, as well as in Africa is traditional and accepted. If you are wearing these items when you are abroad in these countries, just make sure to leave those items in your handbag when you leave those countries (of course there is no given rule book about it) it's just a matter of how you want to be perceived. Your mind may still be in another country, just remember that you are now back in a place or environment which may be of a more formal setting. I'll leave you to figure this one out with your kids after their 'gap year' travels. It may be a tough topic which you just have to 'ride through' and let it take its course, as a parent. One minute you may have a well-dressed lady on your hands, the next time they would have experimented abroad with dress code and discovered that they prefer being a hippy. That is the 'spice of life.'

DATING AS A 'POWER PRINCESS' SHOULD

PART ONE

- Parents never let your girls accept a date for less than what they have been accustomed to. Here are some strong points below on how they can grow to enjoy being on a date or having practice early on with playdates. Initially, as parents, you will more than likely always be open to who they play with. Any parent with sense, will of course have the intuition with not allowing their child's playdate to proceed with the school bully. There are so many aspects to how we go ahead showing your kids who and who is not acceptable to date. Avoiding peer pressure and being polite to the very parent you know very well that their child is bullying yours. You must be strong enough to decline the invite and say that the two of them just unfortunately are not compatible play mates. Then offer to go for coffee with them on their own. This is how your girls should learn to accept an invite with someone they wish to spend their precious energy with, and who are well behaved role models to be around. Perhaps your child is the great role model, or bully, think how you would feel?

- Your little girl may be extremely excited, that is super, let her excitement flow.

- Details on destination is key early on. She can practice letting her tell all the ins and outs of where it's taking place, directly to her friend herself.

- Perhaps the two friends would like to do this together. Two options are enough. If they fight - take charge as parents. Then choose a different venue out of the ones already offered. Try not to undermine them with competition, or just organise the one venue from the start, discussed between the parents.

- Time keeping is especially important.

- Never cancel for another playdate. Arrange it for another day and only tell the child after the first playdate. She may boast and it will lead to competition. There is no need for that. One thing at a time.

DATING AS A 'POWER PRINCESS' SHOULD

PART TWO

- Prepare a dress code for the event if formal. If not, then anything goes. Be mindful if your child is going to the other child's house of a different culture. Discuss beforehand how they must behave and the importance of taking their shoes off at the door. Offer to help and to remember their 'impeccable manners.

- Avoid 'spiteful arguments' as much as possible and try to do their best to include other kids.

- Take a small gift for her friends' family i.e. packet of biscuits or small cake. It does not always need to be homemade. It is the thought that counts and is a great meeting gift of gratification. This also softens the first meeting.

- Always say "thank you so much for having me" once they say goodbye.

- All the above also refers to boys.

- A basic 'rule of thumb' is to dress up for anything elitist, dress down for a party or gathering which is not so elitist. Discuss dress code with the host beforehand. Consider the host and the type of people they are. Just learn to 'fit-in' for at least that brief period. Try not to look the odd one out. Everyone is there to have fun anyway and to enjoy themselves. No need to compete on wealth or status.

THE POWER OF FAMILY VALUES

➡ Values are quite different and vary from family to family. The most important value is security and letting your family know that you will always love them and put them first by being there for them in every way possible. Everything else in life will be able to flow and grow from that. Values are:

➡ Being flexible.

➡ Respecting members of your family and friends.

➡ Being honest with your family and friends.

➡ Being generous and thoughtful.

➡ Communicating well with others and trying to manage your emotions in heated situations.

➡ Being responsible for your actions.

➡ Values are important because a person with no values does not have any respect for themselves or anyone else. How can we have good etiquette as well as having bad values at the same time? Well, we can't. We need values and etiquette to work well together and the best way to do this is to go and practice. No-one is perfect, but the power of holding onto family values as well as being well mannered, takes practice and empathy.

➡ We will always make mistakes, but how we overcome those mistakes is important. Discuss with your kids or classroom how you can overcome any mistakes. Ask them what they value? Ask them what is not of value. You will then be able to help them put things into perspective.

BEHAVIOUR AT HOME

- Parents and teachers - discuss that behaving well extends to all aspects of your life: at home, in the homes of others, on the phone, on the internet and anywhere else. General manners and etiquette should always be respected at home and in the homes of others. Here are some important points of discussion. Be mindful and open with conversation. The first point is what to acknowledge if they are staying over at a friend's home from an unfamiliar cultural heritage. Teach them to enjoy the differences, embrace them and try not to judge.

- Think about their culture first and ask yourself if they behave the same way your family does at home.

- Upon arrival, ask if you should take your shoes off at the door.

- Always be on your best behaviour, remember your manners and general rules of etiquette.

- Do whatever you are asked, even if you don't want to or feel like doing it.

- Don't talk back or be rude to someone when you are a guest in their home.

- Don't scream, shout or run around the house.

- Always offer your help.

- Tidy up after yourself.

- Most importantly, our kids should start by learning these important points from their own home environment. We all know it's not always easy, but a little everyday goes a long way with practicing taking their shoes off as they enter the front door. A lot of cultures are strict about bringing germs into their homes, which shoes do collect on the soles quite regularly.

'POWER BRAINS' - HEALTH AND NUTRITION

➡ Parents and teachers, we can't deny it: Health is everything in life; it comes before our relationships and other areas of our lives. If we do not have our health, then there is no way that we can be the best person that we can be. Get started and act now to enhance your life and give your kids the honour of growing a healthy brain. Start with the right foods. Staying healthy for your mind and your body is everything having a good balance with mental health.

➡ Let us look at what we need to do to eat correctly and be the best person we can be, by being healthy from the inside out:

➡ Exercise at least 30 minutes a day.

➡ Get a good night's sleep, 8 hrs are sufficient.

➡ Laugh! It's proven to make you healthier.

➡ Take at least 15 minutes in your day to close your eyes, relax and do nothing, power naps do the trick!

➡ Eat plenty of fruit and vegetables – at least 5-9 servings a day.

➡ Drink plenty of water.

➡ Do what you love – whether it's boxing, judo or going for a bike ride or dancing, this is good for our mental health.

➡ Create a large project, cut out from magazines, or find foods on the internet the kids can download, print, and stick on the card. You should have two sides. One with healthy food and one with unhealthy food. Discuss good nutrition and obesity. This is a big problem which can lead to all sorts of illnesses. We need to be frank with our kids that nutrition is key to living a healthy lifestyle.

A FEW BASIC FRENCH DINING WORDS TO MASTER

➡ Parents and teachers, we all know that when going to a fancy restaurant, often there are some tricky French words on the menu For those of us who have not put learning French as a priority, will often just gaze at the menu, wondering what on earth they mean, or even, if some of us don't speak the lingo, how on earth to pronounce these words exactly. Really though, these particular words are a wonderful thing to learn and can show a little refinement.

➡ There are a few of these words below, your kids could also hop onto the internet and practice them, just turn up your speaker. So here we go, a little practice goes a long way when sitting at a table. It also gives a good impression that your kids can learn a few basics in a formal dining setting.

➡ Learn PART 1 and then PART 2 in separate stages. Master the first list first then move on to the second.

BASIC FRENCH DINING WORDS

PART 1

➡ Merci – Thank you

➡ à bientôt – See you soon

➡ Bonjour – Hello

➡ N'est-ce pas? – Isn't that so?

➡ Bon Appetit – Enjoy your meal

➡ Petit déjeuner - Breakfast

➡ Diner - Dinner

➡ Dessert - Dessert

➡ Jamon - Ham

➡ Maître d'hôtel – Butler or Head Waiter

BASIC FRENCH DINING WORDS

PART 2

- Hors d'oeuvre - Appetizer
- Fromage - Cheese
- Framboise - Raspberry
- Entrée – Main dish
- Soupe du Jour – Soup of the day
- À la carte – As indicated on the menu
- Sauté – Fried or tossed in the pan
- Prix fixe – Set price
- Grille – Grilled or broiled
- Legumes - Vegetables
- Caviar – Fish roe or Fish eggs
- Répondez s'il vous plaît – Please Reply
- Café au lait – Coffee with milk
- Fraise – Strawberry

THE POWERFUL WORD - 'RESPECT'

- Parents - teach your kids that there are many things you can keep in mind when addressing your peers, adults, teachers, and elderly people that constitute good manners and good etiquette. The way you act and treat people reflects well upon you. You should carry yourself well and treat others with the same respect you would expect from them. Here are some of the things you should remember:

- Be thoughtful and kind – remember to say "please" and "thank you".

- Be thoughtful with your tone and questions – the tone of voice you use is just as important as what you are saying.

- Smile to make others feel comfortable.

- Make eye contact to establish trust.

- Always be thoughtful and kind to the elderly and less able – remember, patience is a virtue.

- Remember your manners.

- Stand when a teacher or parent enters the classroom.

- Never be rude to anyone in public, never be critical, or try to embarrass them.

- Avoid asking questions that are too personal or private, especially in public.

- Be considerate.

- Never interrupt a conversation and wait your turn to speak.

- Do not eat on the street as it is considered vulgar.

- Never shout or swear as it is considered rude and vulgar.

- Discuss this topic with your kids and class, try not to look at the child who is the most disrespectful, like you are pointing out the obvious. Make it a 'team talk.'

THE POWER OF CONFIDENCE

- Lacking confidence and having fears are a natural part of being a human being. We all have times when we are lacking in confidence, are scared, or in need of a boost, so here are some ways to build up your confidence.

- Make three lists: one of your strengths, one of your achievements and one of the things you admire about yourself – keep it safe and whenever you need a boost, read it again.

- Exercise regularly – feeling good and looking good help boost your confidence.

- Dress in a way that makes you feel comfortable and confident but try to look good and well put together.

- Eat well – good healthy food makes you not only feel better physically, you'll also feel full of energy and vitality.

- Get enough sleep – sleep helps manage stress levels.

- Do wonderful things for others.

- Avoid people or places that make you feel bad.

- If you have a problem, seek the advice of an adult or authority figure.

- Spend time with people who value you and your opinion.

- Set yourself challenges as you'll not only learn new things; you'll meet new and exciting people.

WORK WITH YOUR KIDS TO MANAGE FEAR

➡ Here are some important discussions to talk through about the word 'fear', with your kids. There are several ways to manage fear.

➡ Take some time out if you feel upset or fearful. Relaxing helps cleanse your mind and lets you focus on the challenge ahead.

➡ Sometimes, embracing the fear makes it easy to cope with the next bout of fear or anxiety.

➡ Try and think realistically, sometimes the fear you feel is much scarier than the reality.

➡ Visualise – imagine yourself in a place of safety and calm.

➡ Treat yourself once you've overcome over a fearful experience.

➡ Talk to someone – a parent, adult, teacher, or friend. They can help you through your fears by talking about it.

➡ Be responsible – do nothing to harm yourself or anyone around you.

THE BIG SCHOOL INTERVIEW

PART 1

➥ Parents, interviews can be tense and exciting at the same time, and we all need a few tips on how to get through them and show ourselves in the best light possible. These are some things you can do as parents before and during an interview to make sure that your kids are at their best.

➥ A lot of the time, the teachers won't ask all the intense questions below, but preparation is a good thing. This will also help them to get ready for far more intense interviews later in life. You will know when to start practicing with age relevance to your child going into the year above, especially for the 11+ entries into schools. Make sure to always find out from the school before the interview, the type of questions they ask. Ask parents the year ahead what the exam covered, as well as the interview process. Do your digging and find out as much as you can so your kids are ready and feeling confident. A lot of this is down to you and doing your 'homework' first as a parent. We all know how stressful it can be trying to get your kids into the school their heart desires.

➥ Do not be tense

➥ Be open

➥ Stimulate curiosity

➥ Be clean and presentable

➥ Give a firm handshake and maintain eye contact

➥ Smile often

➥ When interviewing for a new school, there are many different questions you may be asked. Here are some of them. Practice the answers and be confident in them.

➥ Why do you want to come to this school?

THE BIG SCHOOL INTERVIEW

PART 2

- What are your strengths and talents?
- How do the subjects we offer match what you plan to learn and study?
- What subjects do you enjoy the most?
- Do you currently take part in any sports or group activities?
- What would you like to achieve in the future?
- What are your hobbies and interests outside of school?
- Do you have a favourite book?
- If you had 2 hours of free time, what would you do with it?
- Do you read a newspaper?
- Do you listen to the news on the radio or watch the news on TV? Try encouraging the child to listen to the radio or watch the daily kids' hour news on TV.
- There are also kids' newspapers. An innovative idea is to get the child to start cutting out bits of interesting news and sticking it in their scrap book once a week for homework. The child, at the end of the session, should stand up and read aloud what they have written and then discuss it with the class or with you as a parent after the activity, or even show it to their teachers at the interview.

SETTING IMPORTANT GOALS

- Goal setting is the opposite of going through life letting things happen to you. If you don't know what you want to achieve out of life, and how you want to succeed in life, you may risk being open to whatever people suggest you do with your life and it won't originally come from you. Goal setting requires you to decide about what you want out of your life.

- Be clear to ask yourself these questions when setting your goals:, Parents and teachers, start by asking the children to ask themselves these questions, depending on your child's age, you will know when they are ready to do this task,

- What is the best way to achieve my goals?

- Can I use any resources to get what I want?

- What skills do I need to learn to best achieve this goal?

- What information do I need and where can I find this information?

- What do I know about this right now and where can I go from here?

- When you know these things, it's time to start actively pursuing these goals but remember:

- Start out small. Big goals can be overwhelming so take it step by step.

- Match your goals to relevant areas of your life.

- Be positive when stating or writing your goals down.

- Don't be tempted to slack off – the fear of failing can stop you from pursuing your goals.

- Write your goals down on paper. This is better than memorising them as you are confirming your willingness to make it come true.

- Read your goals every morning when you wake up.

- Stop 'procrastinating'. This means don't put things off – never do tomorrow what can be done today.

- Really go for your goals and challenge yourself.

- Review your progress and how your goal is being achieved so far.

MASTERING & MANAGING MONEY

PART 1

- Learning about the value of money is incredibly important from an early age. Parents, to give your children early incentives to learn and grow through being rewarded, as the saying goes, 'money makes the world go round'. Understanding the basics of money and how rewarding it can be to receive it, helps our kids to understand the basic principles of how importantly they need to become better savers now and for their future progress in life. We need to start saving from a young age and respect having money when we have it, or it will just disappear if you spend too much of it too quickly.

- What you are going to do, and how you are going to learn how to start saving your money, is through a very basic system that I call the 'Sticky Jar' system. It's fun and informative to do with your kids.

- You will need six glass jars or plastic pots with lids on them. Make sure that they are clean and ready to use for their hard-earned cash to go inside of them!

- And here is what they need to do when they receive rewards for either good homework or great behaviour! Teachers can also use this in the classroom and it could be a joined class system where you start working on a fun way to earn a reward for each child at the end of each week. Of course, if they misbehave and do not use correct etiquette skills correctly or misbehave, then money will be deducted from the class 'sticky jar' pots.

- Write these 'titles' on each label and stick them to your jars. However much money they are given by the parents or relatives doing this at home, you can then divide it up between the six jars.

MASTERING & MANAGING MONEY

PART 2

- ➡ LABEL THE JARS BELOW WITH THE FOLLOWING:

- ➡ FFA - FINANCIAL FREEDOM 'STICKY JAR': This is the jar you are NEVER allowed to spend money from. This is purely a savings jar

- ➡ EDU - EDUCATIONAL 'STICKY JAR': With this jar you only use this for anything educational. Therefore, you won't be spending very much of it

- ➡ LTS - LONG-TERM SAVING FOR SPENDING 'STICKY JAR': Basically this jar is for if you go on holiday, or you would like to save for a big toy, a day out with friends.

- ➡ PLAY - 'STICKY JAR': With this jar you can use it when and as you wish! Have fun and go out and play with the cash from it. Whatever you want to do with it. Just be wise with it.

- ➡ GIVE - 'STICKY JAR': This jar is the charity jar. It is for giving and being thoughtful and kind or lending money to others.

- ➡ NEC - NECESSITY 'STICKY JAR': For paying back loans, food, bills, necessities.

MASTERING & MANAGING MONEY

PART 3

- To make things simpler, you can break up the percentage of your allowance or earnings into six percentage rates.
- FFA – 10%
- EDU – 10%
- LTS – 10%
- PLAY – 10%
- GIVE – 5%
- NEC – 55%

Enjoy the system, it'll help you teach your kids about managing money for when you start saving and having your own strategized and separate bank accounts, to manage your money in this exact order.

HOW TO BE A GREAT ROLE MODEL AND LEADER

➡ Being a leader means setting an example for others, so you always want that example to be a good one. Here are some ways that you as parents and teachers can talk to your kids about what is involved in being a great leader and role model:

➡ Respect others with kindness.

➡ Go for your goals.

➡ Be a great listener.

➡ Be well presented.

➡ Be flexible and helpful.

➡ Never give up.

➡ Adopt a 'can-do' attitude.

➡ Be pleasant, civilised, and courteous always.

➡ As the saying goes "How you do anything is how you do everything!" Being a role model is not just about being the best person you can be, but also trying to encourage others to do the same thing. A role model is someone whose behaviour is imitated or copied by others, so by being a great role model, one has to behave in a way that is an example to others.

➡ Identify the really good bits of your personality that you would like to pass onto others and show how much you are there for them by being caring and thoughtful. Ask your kids to do this task, encourage them to bring out the absolute best in themselves.

➡ Ask your kids to think about what is negative about their thoughts and characteristics and actively try working on ways to improve them. Remember, being a role model doesn't mean you always have the best ideas and answers to everything. Try to understand that there are other paths of action that you can encourage to help others. You also need to 'listen' carefully and take note of what others have to say.

THOUGHTFULNESS - WHAT IS IT?

➡ Parents, we don't need to go into too much depth with this topic, it should be a quick discussion that allows your children to retain these important points in their minds. Being thoughtful, considerate, kind, caring and respectful of others is one of the greatest things you can do for yourself and for those around you.

➡ How you treat and think of others shows how you think of yourself. By following some important guidelines, we can then help others and ourselves to become better people.

➡ Always try and put yourself in other people shoes.

➡ Try and act with compassion and kindness with your friends and family.

➡ Do good things for others without expecting anything in return.

➡ Ask your children what they think are priorities to being thoughtful and kind.

THE POSITIVE STUDENT

- Being a good student is a process and it's not an easy or quick one. One cannot just be a good test taker or show up for class every day and be a good student. Here are just a few ways you can be a good student:

- Have perseverance – things aren't always going to be easy.

- Prioritise your work.

- Listen attentively during class so you never miss anything important.

- Prepare for tests ahead of time and don't procrastinate.

- Come to class prepared – books, paper, pens, pencils, and anything else you'll need.

- Come to class ready to learn.

- Don't play games, talk and slack off when you should be listening, reading or working.

CLASSROOM ETIQUETTE

➡ Parents and teachers, a quick discussion to have with your children, or it just goes 'in through one ear and out the other'...

➡ Don't be rude, cheeky or talk-back to teachers.

➡ Keep noise to a minimum.

➡ Cooperate with the other children in your class.

➡ Don't talk while the teacher is talking.

➡ Don't steal or borrow something from someone without asking.

➡ Pick up after yourself and keep your workspace and classroom tidy.

➡ Wear your uniform with pride and abide by all school dress-code.

PLAY AND PARK AREA RULES

PART 1

- Teachers and parents, Park and play area safety is very crucial to not only the child's behaviour so nothing hurtful or physically painful happens to them or anyone else but even more so their safety from outside intruders! As a teacher or parent, this is a good section to incorporate into being a positive student and how the children can learn and develop structure in their school play area by being on the best behaviour they can be and how to socialise in the correct manner, in the correct parts of the play area by being thoughtful and kind. Also being on the alert for any predators or any person that does not look as though they fit in with the school environment.

- As a practical lesson, you can teach your children/child by taking them to the playground and showing them where is a good place to play and which areas are off limits. For this topic you can go into as much depth as you feel necessary with your child/children, you should know how much discussion your child/children should know by now to go into discussion with them below.

- Once they have listened to you talking, as the teacher, as a practical, act out as a stranger in the school offering the child sweets or a gift or some sort - should they say no or yes to the stranger? Should they run away and get a teacher at once to see who this person is? Should they ever open the gate or the front door for someone who they do not know?

- Keep asking them questions - as a parent, you can go into great depth about his subject. Let's say, just before you take your children on holiday, discuss this topic with them in the car, in the aeroplane or anywhere you feel is right to do so, just make sure you discuss it with them and keep repeating it as much as possible to them every day if you are away on holiday before any outing and how important it is to stay close to you or the carer at all times.

140

PLAY AND PARK AREA RULES

PART 2

- ➡ THE IMPORTANT POINTS THE KIDS MUST KNOW AND UNDERSTAND:

- ➡ Never speak to strangers, no matter how 'nice' they may seem.

- ➡ Remember, if you can't see an adult or a teacher, that means they can't see you so try and maintain a safe distance from them.

- ➡ Don't fight, pull or shove anyone.

- ➡ Don't litter your surroundings.

- ➡ Watch for bullying or fighting and be sure to report it.

- ➡ Don't smoke or do drugs no matter what someone says or who offers it to you (discuss this with the children depending on age).

- ➡ Stay out of areas marked by serious signs of warning.

- ➡ Know your address and phone number by heart in case you get lost.

- ➡ In an emergency, try and find a police officer or security services, or go to the main office if they get lost.

- ➡ Vandalism is forbidden in any play area.

PLANNING AN INFORMAL BIRTHDAY PARTY

➡ Parents, events like birthday parties can be fun and exciting, but making sure they go right is just as important as the event itself. Here are some things you can do to make sure your event, the invitations and festivities go well.

➡ Keep the number of guests small so everyone has an enjoyable time and it's easier to supervise.

➡ Try and arrange the party in the early afternoon into the evening so it doesn't go on too long into the night.

➡ Organise the food so it is ready the day before to keep it as fresh as possible.

➡ Ask the parents of your guests if anyone has any food allergies.

➡ Create a party theme.

➡ Make sure your home or events space is free of any form of dangerous items or things that may cause injury.

PLANNING A BIG BIRTHDAY PARTY

PART 1

➡ Parents, organising a party for kids is not as complex as it sounds, once you understand the basic structure. Fun colours and organised invites require careful preparation. Once you feel your child is old enough to organise their birthday party with you, then you really should, as a parent, sit down with them and go through the planning together, giving them key points for them to work on. This way, your kids will learn how to plan for future events, and what better way is there to do so, by planning their own party with you. My advice is not to try take full control of the situation, share the responsibilities with your kids, show them that what you're doing for them takes preparation, therefore they will learn the art of gratitude, and hopefully appreciate future projects every time you go out of your way to do something nice for them. They will also learn how to structure. With every good structure comes a great planned outcome. Firstly, supervision for a children's party is paramount, from start to finish.

GUESTS & STAFF – Generally speaking, a toddler's party, will not go on for more than 2 hrs at the most.

➡ For a toddler's party, either do it first thing in the morning, from 10 am – 11:30 am or in the afternoon from 2:30 – 4:30 pm (Generally this is the perfect time, so parents, carers etc can get back home into bed time routine asap).

➡ With the older kids, 12 children are enough to create a big party. If you are planning on the whole class to come, I suggest you have parents stay throughout. Therefore, you may need a bigger catering team, or suggest that everyone brings a plate of snacks.

- Always have people willing to help you, parties for children are not easy to manage. I suggest that if parents cannot make it, they must hire a babysitter to watch over their child. Or you could always possibly hire a few temp babysitters to keep an eye on the children. One babysitter to 3 children is required by law here in the UK. So, check local laws in your local area. Always do police background checks on those you hire, even for a brief period. The agencies should have all the details for this before hiring their staff working with kids.

PLANNING A BIG BIRTHDAY PARTY

PART 2

TABLE DECORATIONS - One of the best things you can do, is have a 'bottom drawer' at home, Where over the years you have managed to save lovely bright table cloths, plastic colourful plates, fun cups and generally have all those important brightly coloured utensils etc for your children's yearly birthday parties. Of course, if you have not done this by now, I highly recommend that you do, this will save you time and pennies in the long run.

- Party hats, napkins and masks can be bought separately each year.

- Careful of crackers for the little ones, they are dangerous. So, judge your child's age and when they are ready for party crackers.

- Sparkly sprinkles for the table, then again, be careful of babies and toddlers eating them.

- Helium balloons can be tied to the backs of chairs and at the top of table legs.

- Napkins can be fun and go with the theme of the party. Placed under or next to each plate before eating. Be generous, place the remaining napkins in the middle of the table for juice spills, wiping mucky fingers etc.

- Purchase a few boxes of wet wipes, also to place on the middle of the table, for toddler parties.

DECORATIONS – Balloons, streamers.

- Themes on fairies or pirates etc, you may create panels on which to attach the pictures.

- Pictures and creative artwork of the themed party can be an exercise done with you and the kids together before the big day.

- Lighting should be bright and colourful, no strobe lights or beamers.

PLANNING A BIG BIRTHDAY PARTY

PART 3

ENTERTAINMENT

➡ When it comes to magicians and clowns, it is imperative that you only hire ones who have been recommended by parents and friends, or who you have seen before. Kids can get really scared by these acts and you really don't want the children feeling nervous and going home crying after the event. Bad jokes and terrible performances can ruin a day as well as your friendships with other parents quite quickly.

➡ You may find an entertainer who works with puppets, which is always light and easy for younger children.

➡ The most popular games to have arranged are:

➡ Pass the Parcel. A tip is to make sure to keep ALL this year's left-over wrapping paper, for next year's pass the parcel. You may use newspaper, but only if you painted it beforehand, assorted colours with watered down paint, so that the kids can distinguish which layer to take off.

➡ Treasure hunts. Make sure objects do not post a choking risk, neither do they contain nuts.

➡ Hide and seek, clear away anything dangerous.

➡ Musical chairs, or rather, musical pillows. Try do this with the toddlers than older kids. The older kids tend to get too fussy and upset. At least with toddlers, the adults will just laugh about it, mostly...

➡ Broken telephone.

➡ **ACTIVITIES WHICH CAN BE AT A SEPARATE TABLE**

➡ Face painting (ask a parent or professional face painter to help).

➡ Painting, drawing, stickers, colouring.

➡ Baking or creating decorative biscuits (Do this with a small party group only).

PLANNING A BIG BIRTHDAY PARTY

PART 4

DRESS CODE

➡ Party themes are exciting for kids, a lot goes into the outfit as well as parents buying the themed purchase weeks in advance sometimes. Here are some ideas for themes which can generate something fun.

➡ Cowboys and Indians, fairies, farmyards, Princes and Princesses, cars, trains, their favourite cartoon characters or books, or a passion of theirs they love. The internet will also give you great ideas, so make sure to do your research. Most importantly, ask your child what they would love to have as a theme. Would they like a pool party or perhaps a football party? What us your child's favourite sport? Or superhero?

➡ Always mark the invitation, saying that it is fancy dress code, with no strict rules. Some kids are really not into dress-up, and that's ok. Have a hat or mask set aside on the theme when your guests arrive as the child might suddenly change their minds and won't want them to feel to left out.

PRESENTS – Party bags to take home are a must. Nothing with a risk of choking, nothing with nuts, nothing chemical based.

➡ Make sure to have small gifts for each game won, wrapped and ready.

FOOD - Every culture is different, so prioritise your food how you would normally

➡ Cut anything with a choking risk in half i.e. grapes, baby tomatoes, carrots etc, this is incredibly important.

- Canapes, small sandwiches, biscuits, crisps, fruit, tartlets, cupcakes, brioche, mini sausages, mini pies, hot dogs, sausage rolls, mini pancakes, novelty biscuits and cakes i.e. cats, dogs, horses, pigs, cows, butterflies, balloon cakes, custard creams, ice-cream only at the end (Which must be a surprise, or guaranteed they won't eat the initial banquet first).

- Make sure nuts, eggs, no sugar, no salty foods, and anything which is highly allergic to kids must not be put on the table. Also beware of religious foods i.e. anyone who does not eat pork or similar. Be mindful and ask if anyone has any allergies before the event. It is important to do this. You really don't want a horrible incident to happen on your own doorstep.

- Have a separate table for parents for coffee, teas, and sandwiches. You can also ask the parents to kindly bring a plate of something for the adults table, if you are too busy to prepare it. Most will be happy to do so.

  DRINKS – Milk, fruit juice (little sugar or mixed with water in jugs) fruit milk drinks, hot chocolate (made lukewarm before serving). Mini water bottles.

PLANNING A BIG BIRTHDAY

PART 5

YOUR CHECKLIST MADE EASY

➡ Organise transport or be strict on not being mum's taxi before the big day, you are too busy.

➡ Is the room where you are holding the event, big, bright, and safe?

➡ Have a list of the kids' names and get to know who goes with which parent or carer.

➡ Have spare napkins, nappies, first aid kit, towels, kitchen towel, bee sting ointment available.

➡ Maps on the invitation and address.

➡ Time of start and finish of the party.

➡ Theme of party on invitations.

➡ Address, names, or emails of those selected parents.

➡ If parents are coming and staying for the duration of the party. If so, a separate coffee and snacks table.

➡ Any allergies to be noted.

➡ Who is picking the kids up after the party?

➡ RSVP cards or tear off slips.

➡ How are the invitation getting to the various families, by email, school bag drop-off or personal mail, or by hand at the school gate yourself?

➡ Are you all sorted with table were, glasses, linens, decoration?

➡ Are you going to have a pinata? Always so much fun!

- Are your take home goody bags ready for the kids?
- Have you prepared the birthday cake? With what theme?
- Drinks and snacks.
- Where will the presents corner be and what time will you open them with your child?
- Have you sorted out childcare?

PLANNING A BIG BIRTHDAY

PART 6

SOME OTHER IMPORTANT THINGS TO REMEMBER

- When will you do all the shopping to keep things fresh?

- Do you have a lot of fridge space?

- Have you created a seating plan? Which kids have a good relationship? Who better to seat them next to?

- Have you created the name cards where the kids will be seated? Or will you just let the natural law, or the pecking order play out instead? Can they choose their own seating?

- Who are your staff or helpers?

- Do you have beautiful flower displays, or do you feel that it's not a priority?

- Will your child draw or write out the invitations or will you just buy them to write in?

- All invites must be sent three weeks in advance.

- Informal invites are okay done by phone, text, or email.

- Check all decoration is safe and placed on walls etc only the day before.

- When are you going to wrap your child's presents without wasting time?

- Do you have a thermometer ready?

- Are the winning gifts wrapped?

- Plan on a venue if you are creating party which is large. There is no need to stress yourself out doing this at home. Often, it's much easier at a hotel, hall, club or restaurant where you won't need to be the one clearing up the mess.

- Smaller parties are so much easier done at home.

PLANNING A BIG BIRTHDAY PARTY

PART 7

SECURITY, SAFETY & SUPERVISION – DEPENDING ON THE AGE OF THE KIDS

➡ Make sure you have a room for coats on entry.

➡ Give each child a printed tote bag with their name on it as they arrive, this makes for a great welcoming. Ask them to put their belongings in the bag upon arrival so nothing of theirs get lost. Alternatively, ask the kids to place all their coats, etc in a neat pile where the other kids have put theirs.

➡ Ask for hands to be washed first upon arrival and then use hand sanitizer.

➡ Children under 5 must always be accompanied.

➡ Every child must have a supervisor when in the swimming pool, who knows how to swim.

➡ Have factor 50 kids' sunblock at hand and a few extra hats and towels.

➡ Will you expect shoes off at the entrance to your home?

➡ Lock away medicines and chemicals, garden tools.

➡ Keep animals away from the children, some kids get really scared, as much as you feel you love your pet. They may be allergic.

➡ If you are in a high-rise building, lock windows. Be careful of kids going too near the edge of the balcony

➡ Remove items that post a choking risk, anything made of glass, hot water, boiling kettles, hot stoves, dangerous knives, or utensils. For anything electric use safety plugs in the sockets. Remove sharp cornered furniture, hide, or put away anything of value.

HOW TO WRITE AND SEND THANK YOU LETTERS

- Teaching the child/children to write thankyou cards is such an important topic. The more time that is taken to write a thank you note to each and every child who attended the event then better, not just focusing on birthday events, but also just saying thank you for presents or even having the child over to play. Start by discussing the importance of this with your kids. Teach your children that this it is a very respectful thing to do.

- You will need to find the addresses of the children. The children will also learn how to write on an envelope, where to write and where to fix a stamp. Of course, most things are done by computer these days whereas by doing this it feels much more personal when receiving a letter or thank you card through the post!

- Decide if you would like to type out or hand-write your letter or thank you note – remember, handwriting is more personal.

- Use the same form of address you would when addressing the person face to face (Mr/Dr/Mum/Ma'am/Madam/Ms).

- Write the address on the centre of the envelope.

- Print the name of the addressee (e.g. Miss T. Jones).

- Print the name or the house number, followed by the street (starting on the line below).

- Write the town.

- Print the name of the location in BLOCK CAPITAL LETTERS.

- On the last line, write the postcode.

- Ensure your writing is clear and correct.

- You can write a return address in the top left-hand side of the letter in case the envelope or package needs to be returned.

➡ Stick the stamp on the top right-hand corner of the envelope.

➡ Depending on the size, you can put it in your local red letter box (here in the UK) or take it to a post office if it is too big.

TABLE MANNERS FOR THE PRINCE AND PRINCESS

- Ok parents and teachers, I'm going to make this as simple as possible. Straightforward and easy. Just follow the points below.

- It is up to you as parents and teachers to manage your child's behaviour at the table and at home. It is not possible to get a toddler listening and focusing on every strategy, but as time goes by and your children grow, use these strategies and help them to practice good table etiquette each and every day.

- This won't be a magic 'over-night' solution. I can assure you. Just keep practicing with your kids and make sure that you also practice in front of them, no elbows on the table.

- Here goes, let's just keep it light and simple so that you don't have to read through mounds of irrelevant content to get to the point.

TABLE MANNERS AT HOME

PART 1

- Sit-up straight with a good posture. Sit towards the front edge of your chair. Bottom half on and half off, not slouching back.

- No crossed legs, feet firmly on the floor. Try not to cross your legs under the table. It may knock over glasses if you hit your knees.

- Say your prayers first if necessary.

- Place your napkins immediately on your lap before dinner is served.

- Bring food up to your mouth with the fork or spoon, not chasing the food down to your plate.

- Elbows to the sides, not leaning on the table while eating.

- Elbows on tables only after the full course meal has been served and no more is coming to the table.

- Wrists are acceptable to rest on the edge of the table whilst holding utensils.

- There are far more advanced silver-service dining lessons kids can take, which is extremely valuable, if ever the opportunity arises. They are highly recommended. Silver service dining can be extremely advanced, with many utensils to choose from and knowing where to start can be tricky. I do highly recommend you offer this course to your children, at some stage in their lives. 7 years is a suitable time to start for silver service dining. They are then mature enough to sit out a few hour-long sessions.

TABLE MANNERS AT HOME

PART 2

- Before being seated, remove any bubble-gum etc from your mouth.
- Wash hands well.
- Sit gracefully and do not run to the table.
- Try not to scrape chairs on the floor.
- Sit correctly and again, place napkins on laps at once.
- Pass any food to the right when dishing up.
- Say thank you (a valuable time for parents to hear their kids saying those special, magic words).
- Make sure they are holding their utensils correctly.
- Eat with your mouth closed, no foul-sounding 'lip-smacking' clapping sounds please.
- Discuss happy topics, and do not ask personal questions at the table.
- Your children can fully grasp the glass with the palm of their hands at this stage.
- Once eaten, do not belch at the table.
- Say "please excuse me from the table" and " thank you for a lovely meal".
- Place your napkin under the right side of your plate, picking up the napkin from the centre. Or, offer to take your plate to the kitchen and help with the washing up, or loading the dishwasher.
- Then remove themselves from the table quietly, all whilst slowly pushing in their chair.

- And repeat! Parents and teachers don't forget to do all of this too. They are learning from you. What they see is what they will do.

- If your child is sick, avoid them sitting at the table, and avoid parties and gatherings at all costs. You don't want to be the one who's child infected everyone with a virus. Keep your friends close!

- Blowing of noses must always be done in the bathroom, whether it's at home or in a restaurant. It does not matter what anyone says, no-one is ok with the sound of a runny nose whilst eating, let alone a good old blowing of the nose at the table.

TABLE MANNERS AT HOME

PART 3

➡ While we are ALL guilty of using certain items at the table i.e. mobile phones, there is never a more prominent time to teach our kids not to, this we also need to practice as adults. Here are the big NO NOs which should not be allowed at the table,

➡ Mobile phones, unless you are waiting for an important call. Stress that excuse to kids if needs must.

➡ Dogs and cats are not allowed to beg at the table. If they do, they should go outside or in another room for the duration of the meal.

➡ Laptops, video games, remote controls for the TV. Which, unless there may be a Friday night TV dinner allowed is still a little naughty if you are watching from the table and creates a few unhealthy habits. Perhaps it's best to do this on the sofa, so that there is a clear divide of what sitting at the table stands for. Family time and conversation, really.

➡ Books, magazines, toys. The table is a place for eating and interacting with one another. That's it. No exceptions. As parents and teachers, you must be strict about this.

TABLE MANNERS AT HOME

PART 4

➡ Blowing on food must always be avoided. It not only spreads germs, it is a horrid sound. Wait until your food has cooled down and practice patience.

➡ Eat with self-control, practice to do so. If you are so hungry before an important gathering of guests arrive, quickly have a slice of bread to calm the nerves.

➡ Practice putting any wrappings underneath the rim of either your plate or side plate.

➡ Practice holding knives and forks properly, with index fingers running down, on top of the rim of each knife and fork. This is so important to get right. There is honestly nothing worse than seeing people not knowing how to hold their utensils properly. It honestly gives a terrible impression. Holding utensils with fists is just not correct - just like trying to walk through a revolving door, the wrong way!

➡ Practice only pulling a mouthful of a bread roll from your side plate off at a time, whilst keeping the roll on your plate. Butter only that mouthful at a time. Do not spread it all over the bread roll. This you can start practicing at home with the kids. Let's just remind ourselves how we are going to show the kids to do the same thing. Once they have mastered the basics, they can then go onto learning more formal settings.

FORMAL DINING ETIQUETTE ADVICE

PART 1

→ Helping your child to understand the importance of great "Dining Etiquette" is paramount to good manners. Most of us have been in a restaurant with a friend or family members, about to eat an exquisite meal, when the children from the table next to ours decide to start throwing food across the table, screaming or running around the restaurant.

→ Unfortunately, the same low level of dining etiquette can be seen in adults too. There is nothing worse than having to sit opposite someone when eating a meal who shouts across the table at you, cannot cut a piece of meat properly or continuously slurps their soup for 15 minutes.

FORMAL DINING ETIQUETTE ADVICE

PART 2

- Children need to learn from an early age how to hold a knife and fork correctly, not to shout out across the table to someone occupying a distant chair, or grab the food on their plate with their fingers. Not only does this make the children look badly behaved and uncivilized, it also reflects negatively on the parents in that we believe haven't taught their children proper table manners.

- Young children are very impressionable and eager to learn, therefore there is absolutely no reason why they should not be taught from a young age how to conduct themselves in a proper manner at the dining table. Good dining etiquette is just basic good manners, something that should come naturally from common sense; but sadly this doesn't appear to be the case for many children these days, whose parents are quite happy to sit there and have a conversation with each other whilst their children run riot amongst other diners.

FORMAL DINING ETIQUETTE ADVICE

PART 3

- Badly behaved children reflect negatively on parents in restaurants

- People are judged by their table manners and should make sure they learn the fundamentals of "Silver Service Dining". People will judge you within a few milliseconds of seeing how you conduct yourself and how well your children behave. If the public see badly behaved children in a restaurant, they will not blame the children, but the parents instead. Therefore, not only is good dining etiquette great for the children, it's also good for the public image of the parents and the family as a whole.

THE BASICS OF TEACHING YOUR CHILD FORMAL DINING ETIQUETTE

- For dining etiquette, with you and your kids, you will be best taking the child/children to a restaurant where they can enjoy a three-course meal, beginning with a starter, a main course and then dessert. Children of ages 7 years + will more than likely not eat more than a three-course meal so therefore best to keep it simple, so they are not too full by the end of the three courses.

- Please check with the restaurant first that they will need to have their guest's places made up for a three-course meal, including butter knife and side plate.

- As a parent, you will start by telling your child or children you are working closely with that they will first need to go and wash their hands.

- They will only sit down when everyone is told to do so, or as soon as an adult has sat down first. Of course, if it is family members they can then wait for the elders and parents to find their seating at the table first.

- When everyone has sat down, with you as being the teacher to your kids at the table, you will then show the children the cutlery, which is to start from the outside in, using the outside utensils first. The waiter should bring the menus and offer any drinks.

- At this time the parent should be the one who announces what everyone is drinking, often the person paying will be the person who speaks for everyone at the table and what it is they are eating or drinking first. This is something you will need to make your children understand.

165

HOW TO READ A FORMAL MENU & THE ART OF TABLE DISCUSSION

- As you are looking at the menu options with the children, you can then discuss with them the different prices of different dishes. Try to discuss with them the importance of not ordering something too expensive on the menu, especially if someone else is paying for their meal.

- You as the parent will tell them about what is acceptable and what is not acceptable to discuss at the table during the time. Try to veer away from topics such as politics, religion or any close personal relationship topics of close family members or friends. Safe topics of conversations would be about art galleries, holidays, and the latest adventures you are planning for yourself and friends or concerts and museums. Of course, keeping up with their general knowledge of the world is extremely important, so it is imperative that they know what is going on all around us. Even if it is just one topic of the news every day, this knowledge should be encouraged. Most importantly, it is knowing when to discuss intense topics at the table and when it's inappropriate to do so. As the parent, try to veer towards lighter topics to keep happy family memories when eating out. Avoid getting into heated alterations on who our next PM should be.

- When the child/children are ordering their food, they must focus on saying 'may I' rather than 'can I'. This sounds a lot more formal and polite.

TYPICAL COURSES SERVED IN A FORMAL SETTING

➡ Parents, here are the typical courses to discuss beforehand. Traditional, formal, multi-course meals will consist of several courses served in succession. The more courses a meal has, the smaller the portions of each course will be. A typical six-course meal order may look something like this:

➡ Hot or Cold first course, depending on the season.

➡ Soup Course.

➡ Meat or Fish Course.

➡ Salad Course.

➡ Dessert Course.

➡ Fruit Course.

➡ There are, of course, many variations to this formal order, with some meals being longer, some shorter. For example, depending on the culture, there may be a separate cheese course, or the meal may be preceded by an *amuse bouche* or small *canapés*.

THE BREAD AND BUTTER BASKET

- Parents, teach your kids how to place their bread on their side plate and to break it up into small pieces. Try to not be too greedy with the bread, as they will have a lot of food coming. They will need to learn to butter their bread on their plate and not up in the air. That is bad form. From then onwards the food should arrive at the table.

- Make sure they do not start eating before you start. The head of the table always initiates the first mouthful. They will need to keep their hands below the table until everyone has their food placed in front of them.

- Always pass the breadbasket to the right.

WAITERS AND NAPKINS - IN A FORMAL SETTING

➡ The waiter should serve from the left, with their left hand, and take away from the right, with their right hand. Children do not need to finish all their food if they are starting to feel full with the first course. You may ask the restaurant for child size portions initially. This is all you will need to prepare with the restaurant beforehand.

➡ By this time, napkins should be on laps. If a child requires to go to the loo, they must say "excuse me from the table" and let the head of the table know they are going to the 'ladies' or 'gents'. As adults we would just excuse ourselves and not say these words but of course being children, you will need to know exactly where they are going for safety reasons. The child must place their napkins on their chair when going to the toilets. At the end of their meal, they then place their napkins on the right-hand side of their empty plates.

➡ Never blow a nose with a napkin. Go to the bathroom at once to do so.

FORMAL KNIVES, FORKS AND SOUP-SPOONS

- As the parent you will need to teach your child how to hold their knife and fork correctly. You will also need to teach them how to place their knife and fork together at the end of each meal.

- When eating the soup course, always remember to move your spoon away from you when eating and never to tap it on the side of the bowl. Soup should be scooped from the side of the bowl furthest from you. Always sip the soup and never slurp! Always bring the spoon to your mouth and never lean over the bowl when eating. It is important to eat with all utensils given starting from the outside in. You can practice using all utensils and dinner course plates before you go out to enjoy the real thing. Encourage the child to say 'Bon Appetit' before starting a meal. This is also a wonderful way of making everyone feel good.

- When the meal is done, teach your child to place napkins on the right side of their plate, say "thank you for a lovely meal" and to push their chair in quietly.

- Formal dining etiquette training is far more meticulous than mentioned above. I highly recommend hiring an expert etiquette trainer for more in-depth knowledge of dining etiquette. For now, though, this is enough for parents to practice with and to manage their children's behaviour in a restaurant primarily. That is a big enough job in itself.

CONQUERING TRICKY & MESSY FOODS

PART 1

Parents, I'll keep this simple. No need to bore you with too many details. This is how it's done and so let's just keep it to the point. You will need to manage your kids' manners based on being patient.

- THE HAMBURGER – Cut it in half. Using fingers is fine. In a formal setting use a knife and fork. Take a slice or bite of the corner first. Have napkins ready.

- FISH-BONES, OLIVE-PIPS AND SEEDS – When removing these from your mouth, cup your hands over the lips, remove and place on side of plate when no-one is looking. You can also practice using a spoon rather than fingers, still cupping your mouth at the same time. Now that is a skill of formality.

- CHIPS (FRENCH FRIES)- Fingers are no problem at all to eat chips, only one or two at a time. If you are in a formal setting, use a knife and fork.

- SAUCES – Place on the top right-hand corner of your plate. If you are left-handed, on the top left.

- LEMONS- Squeeze gently. Cup one hand over it as you squeeze.

- ASPARAGUS- Use a knife and fork. Fingers use minimally. Chop away the hard part of the stem.

- SALAD – This may come before or with the entree. With a salad fork and knife, cut the salad. Slowly slice cherry tomatoes with a sharp knife, or if small enough let them pop in your mouth, whole. Try not to look like a chipmunk, it's never a good look.

➡ CONDIMENTS- Place only one teaspoon at a time to the side of the plate. Never baste it on top of the food. Try not to tap your plate when placing it there. This should be done silently.

➡ SALT AND PEPPER- They are a team, if someone asks you for the pepper, always pass the salt and pepper pots together, they are best friends and never apart. Pass to your right and not across the table in a formal restaurant.

CONQUERING TRICKY & MESSY FOODS

PART 2

- ➡ SPAGHETTI- Tines of the fork are placed into a few strands of spaghetti to the side of the bowl. Practice twirling. Use a dessert spoon to twist the spaghetti if tricky. Keep it placed on the bottom of the plate, not in the air. Any floating strands may get bitten off to drop into the plate. This is quite an art to achieve, it takes practice. Take in only enough for a small mouthful. We all know how large our twirls of spaghetti can become!

- ➡ SOUP – NO SLURPING – Move the spoon away from you towards the back of your bowl. Once finished, place your spoon on the plate underneath to the right-hand side. Or if there is no plate, leave it in the bowl to the right.

- ➡ LOBSTER – Requires a big nutcracker and a lobster fork. Hold with one hand, use the nutcracker to crack the lobster with the other hand, close to the joint of the lobster. Use the lobster fork to pull the lobster meat out of the tricky areas of the lobster claw. Crack slowly so no juices squirt across the table. Cut the meat, dip it into the butter sauce provided. The tomalley and red roe are considered THE delicacies in the female lobster. Try them, you never know, you might find them delicious. A finger bowl is needed, and plenty of napkins.

- ➡ SKEWER- Place it upright on the plate. Slide a few pieces of meat or vegetables off at a time. Place skewer at the top of your plate as you eat. Cut the meat and enjoy.

- ➡ PIZZA- At home eat it with your hands. When in a formal setting, use a knife and fork.

- ➡ FRUIT- At home, you can eat with fingers. In a formal restaurant where the fruit is already sliced, either use a knife and fork. Or alternatively, if it's a fruit salad, use a spoon.

- CORN ON THE COB- At home use fingers, no problem. When in a formal restaurant, place the corn on the cob on its flat side, use a sharp knife to slice away the corn from the cob away from the sides, using your fork to keep it steady from the top flat surface.

- FISH ON THE BONE – Use your fish knife to slowly remove the fish flesh away from the bone, using the edge or side of the fish knife in the same direction as the bone, towards the top of the fish. If the fish has skin, use your fish knife to pull it away beforehand. Keep skin and bones neatly on the top right-hand corner of the plate.

- FRIED CHICKEN- At home, by all means use your fingers, or in a takeaway shop that is also accepted. In a formal restaurant use a knife and fork. Don't suck on the chicken bones. Place bones on top right-hand corner of your plate neatly.

- These are the basic tricky foods which kids mostly will eat. Work on these first before mastering other tricky foods. There are many more which you could always look up on the internet and practice conquering, as and when.

- ARTICHOKE- With your class or kids, your task is to do your research on how to eat an artichoke. This is tricky for kids and a real art! It can be eaten hot or cold.

CHOPSTICKS ETIQUETTE

PART 1

- Parents and teachers, chopsticks are an art! They are tricky to hold but so much fun to use! Done correctly though, is a different story, and so is your general etiquette when it comes to using them in a Chinese restaurant. The Chinese are very proud of their heritage and just like Western dining, the Chinese are very particular on how you not only hold your chopsticks, but also your general etiquette and mannerisms when eating. It would be exactly the same for them going to a formal restaurant and not knowing how to hold a knife and fork properly, which is common, as they don't generally use knives and forks like we do. Therefore, it is important to practice with chopsticks. You do get the disposable chopsticks and the chopsticks which have their own small holders, which are washed like knives and forks after every meal. Here are some wonderful tips to focus on with your kids at home or in a Chinese restaurant.

- Picking up the bowl with your hands to push food into your mouth with chopsticks, is acceptable.

- Piercing your food with chopsticks is considered very rude!

- Pointing your chopsticks at people when talking and making a point is considered very rude!

- Never put your chopsticks into a bowl of rice. This is considered very rude! Use the spoon provided.

- Never leave your chopsticks pointing directly at someone across the table, this is considered very rude! Angle them slightly, or balance them on their holder, parallel to your body.

- Never wave them in the air, keep them low to the table.

- Eating with a spoon is better than a knife and fork, if you find chopsticks impossible to use.

- In China burping at the table is considered a compliment to the chef. Whereas in Japan, like us Westerners, is considered very rude!

- Always keep your chopsticks together when not in use. They are considered a team.

- Only ever use your chopsticks to pull out bones from your mouth or use your fingers. Never spit them out on the plate.

- Never use chopsticks to pick up large and slippery food.

- Never use mismatched chopsticks in length or look. Get them changed immediately or it means misfortune is on its way.

CHOP-STICKS ETIQUETTE

PART 2

- Chopsticks are purely for food. Never to pick-up anything else.
- Never click your chopsticks together, this is considered very rude!
- Slurping noodles is considered not to be rude but a compliment to the chef.
- Never suck your sauce or rice grains off the end of chopsticks, this is considered very rude!
- Chopsticks should be placed above the bowl, parallel to the table when you have finished.
- The tips of chopsticks must always face to the left of you.
- Never rub chopsticks which are disposable together, it implies that they are cheap to the restaurant owners and this is considered very rude!
- By leaving your chopsticks stuck directly and vertically in your food, this implies death. Never do it. Place your chopsticks down on their holder or at the top of your bowl parallel to you, when not in use. Standing vertically in the bowl brings bad luck!
- Never play drumsticks with your chopsticks, this is considered very rude!
- When passing dishes around the table, always place your chopsticks back on their holder or parallel at the top of your plate or bowl, ends pointed left. Never keep them in your mouth.
- Only ever use the serving chopsticks or spoons provided to dish-up onto your own plate. Never your own chopsticks. The same principle as the West - hygiene comes first.

- Never push the bowls on the table around with chopsticks.

- In China, always leave some food in your plate when you are finished. If you don't do this practice it implies to your host that they did not feed you enough. When in Japan it is the total opposite. Make sure to finish to the last grain.

- Dropping your chopsticks on the floor is said to bring bad luck.

- HOW DO YOU USE CHOPSTICKS? WITH PRACTICE. Hold the upper chopstick like you would a fork or pencil, about one-third down from the top of the chopstick. Place second finger (ring finger) with base of your thumb. All pointing fingers the same way. Move the chopstick above, with your thumb, your index and middle finger.

BIG TIPS ON CULTURAL ETIQUETTE

- We are going to cover a few major cultures and their etiquette rules. These are always handy to know and teach your children about how all cultures are different. They should learn to have the understanding and appreciation that all things far and wide are a mark of our heritage. The main rule to follow when meeting or interacting with people from diverse cultures is to research their customs and have a general understanding of their culture. By doing this, you'll be sure that you won't do anything that might offend them. Always abide by their rules. Some countries are extremely strict, and if you don't follow their protocol, you could end up in trouble with their law.

- Some of the things you can learn by researching the various aspects of cultures you may encounter are:

- How to meet and greet people.

- How to assess body language.

- Know how to dine with them.

- Know how to treat their home and belongings.

- Understand how they interact with friends and family members.

- So much more!

- Only by doing the appropriate research can you be sure that your next interaction with someone from a culture different than yours will go smoothly and you will leave a great and lasting impression on them.

- So, let us start with our own culture - Great Britain.

BIG TIPS ON CULTURAL ETIQUETTE

GREAT BRITAIN

- 'English' and 'British' do not mean the same thing. 'English' refers to people from England. 'British' refers to people from England, Scotland, Northern Ireland, or Wales.

- Try not to confuse countries people may be from

- The British are more reserved in their body language

- If invited to someone's home, it is normal to bring a gift of chocolates or flowers

- The British value being on time

- Table manners are Continental

- Do not rest your elbows on the table

- A firm handshake is normal for both males and females

- Wait until you are invited to refer to someone by their first name

- Take your hat off when you go indoors (for males)

- Women can keep their hats on indoors except whilst at a table or in a church

- Always remove your hat around your elders

- Say 'excuse me' when passing by someone or wanting to interrupt a conversation in a group setting

BIG TIPS ON CULTURAL ETIQUETTE

SOUTH AMERICA/ARGENTINA

- Spanish is the predominant language spoken
- There are 17 Native languages
- One of traditional and most popular dances is the tango
- Sport is extremely important
- Argentinians love to be out at night
- 93% are Roman Catholic
- Standing straight and keeping your hands out of your pockets are signs of good manners
- Hands on your hips is considered confrontational and rude
- European table manners are the norm

BIG TIPS ON CULTURAL ETIQUETTE

AFRICA/ SOUTH AFRICA

- English is the official language of the government and secondary education system
- There are many Whites and Indians in South Africa, as well as Africans
- Western dress is common in most areas of South Africa
- Always be punctual
- Failing to greet someone is considered very rude
- A foreigner should wait to be introduced
- When offering or accepting objects, do so with both hands
- Never give or accept anything with your left hand
- Eat with your right hand
- Never smell the food while it is cooking or when it is being served
- Leave a little food on the plate to indicate that the meal has been filling

BIG TIPS ON CULTURAL ETIQUETTE

ASIA/CHINA

- The four major dialects are Cantonese, Shanghainese, Fukienese and Hakka

- China is the 3rd largest country in the world, with a population of over 1.2 billion

- There is no official religion, but Buddhism is extremely popular

- The dress code is generally traditional and neat

- Women should wear skirts on the knee or below, with minimal make-up

- Avoid wearing solid red, solid black, or white

- Always be punctual

- With foreigners a handshake is offered when greeting, but lower your eyes and do not make direct eye contact for too long

- Always show respect for the opinion of others who are older or of senior position

- When passing a plate or drink, do so with both hands

- Shoes are always removed when entering a house

- Always bow to say hello, and goodbye

BIG TIPS ON CULTURAL ETIQUETTE

EUROPE/GERMANY/ SWITZERLAND

- After Russian, German is the most frequently spoken language in Europe

- Germans and most Europeans see themselves as rational and disciplined

- Europeans appreciate punctuality, privacy, and skill

- Being natural equates to being 'honest' as opposed to 'false'

- Germans and Russians may appear slightly aggressive, but they also have a sense of humour

- Europeans value education and culture

- German/Russian women tend to wear elegant tailored clothing

- Men tend to be conservative

- When entering an establishment, it is customary to greet people and say goodbye when leaving

- Always shake hands at the beginning and at the end when meeting new people

- Germans are extremely quiet during a performance

- Never buy gifts that are personal (perfume, soap, or clothing)

- English style of table manners is the norm

- Leaving food on your plate is considered wasteful

- Germans believe content is more important than style

BIG TIPS ON CULTURAL ETIQUETTE

UNITED ARAB EMIRATES (UAE)
PART 1

- Arabic is the official language
- English is widely understood and used in business
- The discovery of oil has brought incredible wealth and new occupations
- Family stability is one of the major goals in life
- Islam is the official religion
- Never place a Qur'an on the floor, on top or amongst other books
- How you dress reflects your status and wealth
- Men should never be bare-chested in public
- Women should not wear revealing clothing
- Always stand to greet someone and whenever someone enters a room
- A handshake should be short and firm and always with the right hand
- Touch your heart with the palm of your right hand after shaking hands

BIG TIPS ON CULTURAL ETIQUETTE

UNITED ARAB EMIRATES (UAE)
PART 2

- It is against religious beliefs for a woman to touch any man other than her husband

- Western women will occasionally find men will not extend their hands to shake

- Men and women do not kiss in public, even if they are married

- Pointing is impolite

- It is impolite to pass in front of someone who is praying

- It is impolite to refuse a gift

- Eat only with your right hand

- It is polite to take a second or third helping but do not leave your plate completely empty

- Be careful of openly admiring your host's ornaments or other belongings as it is an Arab custom to make a gift of anything a guest admires

BIG TIPS ON CULTURAL ETIQUETTE

SPAIN

- There are four official languages: Castilian spoken by 74% of the population, Catalan, Galician, and Basque spoken by the rest
- English and French are the most common second and third languages
- The family is the backbone of Spanish society
- Spaniards hold an extraordinarily strong work ethic
- Spain is historically Roman Catholic
- Personal pride and appearance are extremely important
- Do not be surprised or offended if your meeting is cancelled at the last minute; being on time is more the exception than the rule
- Eye contact is important and is often held longer than in other cultures
- Yawning or stretching in formal situations is unacceptable
- If you are given a gift open it immediately
- Spaniards like to take time when eating and drinking

BIG TIPS ON CULTURAL ETIQUETTE

WEST AFRICA

- The official language of Senegal is French
- There are also six additional major languages spoken in Senegal
- After the Ivory Coast, Senegal has the most developed manufacturing sector in West Africa
- In the North where Muslims tend to be from, women should wear skirts below the knee
- White women should not wear their hair in cornrows as it is considered disrespectful to black Senegalese women
- Not greeting someone when meeting them is considered rude
- As a foreigner, always wait to be introduced
- Never introduce yourself to the Chief of the village
- Do not shake hands with a Senegalese woman unless she extends her hand first
- Looking people in the eye is often a good moral practice
- Food is normally eaten with your fingers
- Senegalese talk little while eating
- Your host will be pleased if you eat a lot, and then leave a little food in the bowl or on your plate

BIG TIPS ON CULTURAL ETIQUETTE

ITALY

- Italian is the official language of Italy
- In Italy, the main priority of life is family
- Status in Italy depends on class, rather than wealth
- Italy is predominantly a Roman Catholic society
- Italians take pride in their appearance, and rarely appear dirty or sloppy
- Italians tend to base their opinions on how you dress
- Always stand when an older person enters the room
- A kiss on each cheek is a greeting in Italy
- Italians can become louder in emotional situations
- If you receive a gift, ask before opening it
- Never eat before the hostess does
- Do not speak ill of religion or sporting teams
- Do not ask a new acquaintance what they do for a living

BIG TIPS ON CULTURAL ETIQUETTE

MALAYSIA

PART 1

- Malay is the language spoken most

- English is the language of business and tourism

- Being polite, considerate, and courteous, is valuable

- Remove your shoes when entering a mosque

- When visiting a Chinese temple, men must remove their hats

- Use the right door for entry, the left door for exit

- It is is customary for both men and women to stand when an elderly person walks through the door

- Bow when meeting, greeting, or passing a group or friend to say "hello"

- Muslim woman will nod to say "hello", they do not touch hands with men

- It is very rude to point

- Do not stand with your hands on your hips

- When sitting do not fold your legs

- Do not pat the head of adults or children, as the head is considered a sacred part of the body

BIG TIPS ON CULTURAL ETIQUETTE

MALAYSIA
PART 2

- Do not blow your nose in front of people
- Asians tend to laugh when they are embarrassed or shy
- Do not open a gift in front of the person who gave it to you
- Eat food with your right hand and drink with your left
- Always finish the rice on your plate but leave a little other food or drink unfinished
- The host will tell you where to sit
- Never take food from another's plate
- Expect to be offered second or third helpings

BIG TIPS ON CULTURAL ETIQUETTE

INDIA
PART 1

- Up to 15 official languages are spoken in India and more than 1,000 minor languages

- The country is divided into states on a linguistic basis

- Hindi is promoted as the national language

- English is widely spoken on a governance scale

- Religion is important in every aspect of Indian life

- Hinduism is India's major religion, followed by about 80% of the population

- Woman traditionally wear a Sari

- The dot (bhindi) worn on the forehead of all Hindu women and some Sikhs is an adornment

- Black is the colour traditionally worn by most unmarried women

- Wearing loose/baggy clothes is advisable for foreigners and women

- Always take off shoes when entering a temple, and women must cover their legs and shoulders fully

- When an older person enters the room, always rise

- Greet family members according to age, older people first.

BIG TIPS ON CULTURAL ETIQUETTE

INDIA
PART 2

- When being introduced to a woman, allow her to make the first move
- Refrain from hugging the person from the opposite sex when greeting
- Only people of the same gender can hug each other
- Never put your hands on an adult's head
- Never sit with the soles of your feet facing another person. It is considered rude
- Do not whistle
- Pointing is rude
- When invited to a meal, bring flowers
- Sexes may be segregated at a meal
- Men will always speak to men and women will speak to women when dining
- Wash hands before and after eating
- Always eat with your right hand
- Never spill your food or lick your fingers
- Always use your left hand to pass things, as your right will be greasy and sticky
- Never offer someone food from your own plate
- At a Muslim Indians home, there may be a prayer rug on the floor. Do not sit or step on it.

THE POWER OF TEA

- Parents and teachers, since tea is such a big part of our history, it is imperative that our kids learn at least a little history on the subject, which really does make a great discussion, over a cup of tea! British people have enjoyed drinking tea for over 350 years. The historical roots of tea go back to China, where it was first discovered. It originated in the mountains of Sichuan and Yunnan, and, according to legend, the earliest Emperor Shen Nung first sampled the drink when some unidentified leaves fell into his pot of hot water. Allegedly, Shen Nung used to wander the country recording the effects of infusions made from the leaves and berries of various plants. He discovered that tea cured him of a stomach-ache contracted because of drinking a toxic herb. Tea has brought people and family gatherings together for over 5,000 years and is the second most consumed beverage after water. There are three basic types of tea:

- Black tea which is popular in Europe and the USA.

- Green tea which is a staple of the Orient.

- Oolong tea which is a cross between the two in flavour and taste.

- Afternoon tea is an English institution, accompanied by sandwiches, scones or cake. India is responsible for cultivating much of the world's tea, and Indian varieties such as Darjeeling, Assam and Nilgiri are amongst the most popular. Discuss the beauty of tea and how various cultures make and blend their tea. What sort of mugs do they drink it from? There is much to find on the internet, you can create a whole project. When I was at school (Taryn Jahme, yes me) I did a project on tea. I was 8 years old. My father was also a tea farmer, so you can understand my passion!

TEACH YOUR KIDS ABOUT TEA BEFORE TEACHING THEM ABOUT FINE WINE

- Of course, it is always important to go through the history of tea with your child/kids. There are so many fun elements to this topic and how you can enjoy experimenting with diverse types of teas from around the world. As the teacher or parent, you should:

- Buy various tealeaves from a teashop, with different flavours and from various parts of the world.

- Discuss the history of tea, look on the internet for video clips on how it is grown and picked in different countries, all the way from India to Africa and other places that enjoy adding honey, milk and different spices to tea.

- Experiment making your own tea by using mint leaves in hot water - always remember your health and safety with kids, as you don't want anyone getting burnt!

- Place all the different types of leaves or tea you have purchased on the table, perhaps ask the kids to bring along some tea cakes to create a small tea party for all to enjoy.

- Go over the different names of tea and where they come from. Taste the different types of teas, give each child a mug to sip on and pour only a little of each at a time for the kids to sample. Make sure they do not burn their mouths.

- You may go on the internet and see how tea is grown, how they dry it out in factories and package the tea to send off to different parts of the globe. Kids must understand that a lot of arduous work goes into growing tea and then getting it ready for consumers.

➡ A little about me. I grew up on a tea farm in central Africa, where my father owned thousands of hectares of tea. My fascination with tea goes back years. I also did a project on tea as a kid and I am truly passionate about the subject. We should all be teaching our kids of the incredible health benefits and fascinating history of tea. Dedicate some time to learn about tea before we subject our pallets to wine! Tea is a super topic to teach our kids.

HIGH TEA

YOUR INVITATION

➡ Parents and teachers, how exciting is it to get an invite to attend a high tea party? Kids absolutely love going for high tea. The fantasy of being back in Alice in Wonderland or dressing up to attend a party at an exclusive hotel for high tea is just as exciting for your kids, as it is for you and I. Honestly, who doesn't love eating scones and jam with perfectly cut triangular sandwiches, off a mountain of plates. There are so many high-end hotels these days which offer amazing deals. High tea today is not just for the elite, it is for everyone to love and enjoy. The excitement can override the event itself for kids, so we do need to abide by some etiquette rules, and these rules your kids should learn early. These are rules for all of us when going for high tea at an exclusive hotel, or cafe. We all want to share these exciting treats off the cake stand together, and so should understand the meaning of the word 'sharing'.

➡ Firstly, if you are off to a formal event with the children, make sure that you make them a small bite to eat at home before you head off to the event or party. This helps your kids to slow down and not have guests staring at you with beady eyes from across the table.

AFTERNOON TEA

- Parents, timing is everything. Don't miss your time slot for high tea at the venue. Do remember that these times throughout the day get booked up quickly. The restaurant must think about their dinner preparations, so make sure to be on time, always.

- Tea is served all day. Allow the host to choose a time.

- As a standard, 4 pm is an appropriate time to book.

- Breakfast tea is in the morning, 12 pm is mid-day tea, Noon tea is at noon.

THE TEACUP AND SAUCER

- Parents, there are so many people who get confused with this. No, you never stick out your little pinkie finger. Never.

- How should you hold a teacup exactly? Hold it so you don't drop it.

- Hold the handle gently with fingers inwards.

- If too hot, be patient and allow it to cool down.

- Never slurp. Ever.

- If you are in a hurry, ask the waiter for some ice, pop a cube into your tea. Sip slowly after a few gentle blows into the cup.

- Cover your hand, cup your palm, and try not to blow over the teacup. Blow into the teacup.

- Always look into your teacup when drinking tea, not over.

- Keep the saucer on the table whilst you sip on your tea, placing the teacup back down in between sips. Never pick up the saucer.

- Your teaspoon should be placed to the right side on the saucer.

- NEVER clink your teaspoon on the rim of your teacup.

- When stirring, NEVER allow the teaspoon to clink the inside of the teacup. No sound should be heard at all. Time to practice!

- Only ever use sugar tongs to pick up the sugar cubes, and lemons. The right utensils will be provided. Keep them where they belong. No-one wants gooey sugar from the lemon bowl.

HIGH-TEA, THE BIG TIPS

- Always add sugar before the teacup is full, and before lemon or milk.

- Pour your tea after adding milk, lemon, or sugar.

- Never have milk and lemon together. Lemon 'splits' the milk, curdling it in the process.

- Put the extra lemon slice on the side of your saucer in case you would like to use it later.

- Never use your fingers to pick up the lemon.

- Take no more than three cakes and sandwiches at once from the cake stand.

- Eat slowly, everyone needs to share, and your kids must know not to finger all the food. Take what you touch. Choose with the eyes first, then proceed.

- Cups, saucers, and plates are removed once everyone has eaten.

- A two-hour timeslot for this gathering is long enough. Don't push with time over that as the kitchen may have to end your stay and ask you to leave, which is sometimes quite embarrassing.

- As parents, watch your alcohol intake, only a couple of glasses of champagne if needs must. Remember where you are, whether a formal setting or not.

- The guest of honour always sits to the right of the main host. The guest of honour is the one to first exit the building.

- No need for thank you cards. A wonderful thank you upon exit is enough.

- Presents and cards are opened after high tea is served and all the plates have been removed.

- Often your child may be extremely excited to receive her/his gifts. Depending on the child's age, restraint is a good thing for them to learn. If they are young and just can't hold on, let them open the presents as the guests arrive. Try not to make the event strained. Allow the excitement and flow of the day to unfold. No need to make anyone feel disappointed. If of course your child's behaviour is just coming across as spoilt, then definitely lay down the restrictions so they don't ruin the day.

WHO POURS THE TEA?

- During your special occasion, the host will pour the tea first. They will then leave the spout of the teapot facing them, once poured.

- The host will be the one closest to the tray or area with the teapot, teacups, and saucers. They will ask the waiter to place it closer to them.

- Remember sugar, milk and lemon goes into the bottom of the teacup first.

- The host will ask everyone, starting with the guest of honour first, how they would like their tea.

- The host will be a great role-model, showing the children how to offer a cup of tea to each guest.

- How do you like your tea? Would you like milk, lemon, or sugar? How many sugars do you take?

- After the guest and the host have conversed, the host will say, "You are most welcome," after the guest has said their thank you, once the teacup and saucer has been served.

- You can encourage your child to help you pour the tea if they are capable enough. Just be careful they don't burn themselves, perhaps at this point it is best that the host pours, the kids can use the tongs for the easy stuff i.e. the lemons, milk, and adding the sugar cubes. The parent, or host can serve the teacups. You don't want your child getting burnt before the party has even started. They can practice with more caution, carrying teacups for you when you are back in your home environment.

- Once the host is settled with her/his tea, and if one of the other parents or guests have already finished, they will have to wait before diving into the tea pot again. Restraint, as everyone needs to share.

Everyone must practice the art of sharing, especially the children. So, whoever is guiding the child, must be firm with them that the cake stand is there for everyone to eat and enjoy.

➡ After everyone has finished their first cup of tea, another round offered and served by the host.

➡ Guests can enjoy wearing hats to the tea-party. Dress code is never formal but smart-casual. Depending on the venue, as a lady or young girl, wearing a lovely day dress, which is not provocative in anyway, is required. Boys can wear chinos and a button up collared shirt.

➡ Dressing to look 'proper' is key.

➡ Invitations can be made via mobile phone or email, a week in advance at the latest.

MOBILE PHONE ETIQUETTE

➡ Parents and teachers, we are ALL guilty of this life's new pleasure, sadly. Gone are the days where sending a letter or using a telegram or a landline was enough. Technology has advanced at such speed, and our children are moving much faster than even we are as adults, with understanding technology. Should we be nervous, yes and no. Mobile phones are pretty much 'the life blood' of our daily living habits, and nothing can rip us apart from these devices which keep us all connected. Yes, this is a tough topic to grasp, but necessary to learn the correct behaviour to manage these devices - especially now that our own children are relying on them increasingly.

➡ What happened to the days when we just knew and trusted that the baby sitter and teachers all had our children in good hands, and we weren't calling them up every hour of each day, asking them mundane questions like, "are you sure they went to bed on time". "Yes, of course they did" said the babysitter, "your child has been perfect". Honestly? We have become too reliant on our mobile phones and technology, which has made technology into our new reality. I see a lot of parents over the years use tech so much, that they almost treat their kids in the same way. If they are not doing something fast enough, like going to brush their teeth, or running to the table directly after school to do their homework, then it's just not good enough.

➡ What has happened to us? It's almost like we are turning our children into AI robots. The reality is no-one works this way. Technology is the fast-paced solution, not children. As parents and teachers, we all need to think about this, take a step back and realise that your kids deserve your 'real time.' And that comes with boundaries, not just with them, but with all of us adults (parents) showing them when it is proper to use a mobile device, and when it's not. Your children deserve real memories with you as a 'real time parent,' yes? Not thoughts of you

sitting on your mobile phone all the time, when the teacher asked them what they did with you over the weekend. These years move fast, before you know it, your kids will be flying the nest and you will be wondering where those years went so fast. Well, it went on your mobile phone.

➡ So here are some mobile etiquette rules, which we can all practice, before it's too late.

WHEN AND WHEN NOT TO USE A MOBILE PHONE

- In an emergency use a mobile phone if you are out with your children or in a meeting.

- Always put your phone on silent or vibrate when you are with others.

- If the call cannot be ignored, exit the room to have your discussion.

- Always take your phone with you if you leave a room.

- In restaurants, phones should be put on silent or turned off. If it's nothing important, the person can wait for your return call.

- Always make the person you are with the priority, not the caller. Unless it's important, you can always send the call to voice message.

- Don't speak on the phone while paying a cashier at the same time.

- Don't shout on the mobile phone.

- Do not argue in public on a mobile. Even with your spouse and especially in front of your kids. Or other parents' kids in fact.

- Don't stand there on your mobile yapping away in the school waiting area. If you are too loud and are more than likely annoying people with your loud voice, this will stop others in conversation.

- Walking around and jabbering away with Bluetooth stuck to your ear really does look ridiculous.

- These are the venues where you must never use a mobile phone, teach your kids that in certain places, mobiles phones are not allowed, only silence. Places of worship, doctor or dentist waiting rooms, libraries, museums, lifts, cinema, cemeteries, theatres and restaurants, public transport where every-one is confined to a small space.

➡ Buses and trains - you may have a quick conversation and say you will call them back once you have hopped off. There is nothing more annoying than someone speaking loudly behind you on your hour journey, all the way to work. Especially if you don't understand their language.

➡ Always turn off sound when around others and playing games on your phone.

➡ Turn off the texting sound on all the buttons, no need for them.

➡ Do not leave phones on restaurant tables at any time.

➡ Keep your texts short and simple. Using the text messaging service is wonderful, as much as it is a curse.

➡ Look out for any signs banning mobile phones.

➡ Always try to be kind. Avoid cyberbullying at all costs.

THE BIG DINING TABLE 'NO-NO'S'

➡ Parents and teachers. Please be mindful of these important 'NO NOs' at the table. You should be firm with your kids on the points below.

➡ Never swing on the chair or tilt your chair backwards and forwards. Especially in a restaurant.

➡ Never pickup your utensils off the floor, if by mistake they fell. The waiter should be called for a new utensil, they will automatically be the ones to pick up the utensil. Say thank you.

➡ How you treat the waiter says a lot about your own character. Be nice.

➡ The back of the chair in the restaurant, is not for you to slouch or rest your arms. No-one wants to see sweaty armpits either. Keep your arms by your sides.

➡ NEVER lick your knife and fork.

➡ Eating with your elbows on the table is a big NO NO.

➡ Do not take mobile phone calls at the table. Especially halfway through a meal. This is the height of rudeness, unless extremely important.

➡ Try not to reach across the table. Ask for the salt and pepper to be passed to you.

➡ Always pass the breadbasket to the right, never to the left of the table.

➡ If you are left-handed, never rearrange the cutlery, just swap each of the utensils around, as and when each course arrives.

➡ Do not speak to others pointing your fork or knife at them or waving your utensils in the air. Place them back on your plate.

➡ Never speak with your mouth full of food. Finish. Then speak. Do not hurry if you have a mouthful when asked a question. If you do happen to mess up, put your hand over your mouth if you say something by mistake, or it's urgent.

- Never drop your napkin on the floor. If you need the loo make sure to leave the napkin on the chair seat, which indicates to the waiter that you will be back. When you have finished your full meal, then leave the napkin tucked to the right-hand side of your plate, or desert bowl.

- NEVER brush your hair, file, or clean your nails or put on your makeup at the table.

- Don't use your napkin to blow your nose. Or as a bib.

- Always use the serving spoons for that dish.

- Never push your dish away from you when in a formal dining room. Don't blow your food, wait a few minutes for it to cool down.

- Don't ask to share food or a desert.

- Don't share utensils or glasses.

- Do not use a toothpick at the table. Take it to the bathroom and clean your teeth there if out.

CONVERSATIONS & LISTENING SKILLS

➡ Parents and teachers? Are you listening to your kids when they have something important to say? Are you overriding their emotions with your own frustrations and emotional outbursts on occasion? Yes, you are, we all know this, we all do this, and how are we going to start to manage ourselves?

➡ Let's get to the point. Without teaching our kids the art of conversation, or how to listen, or in fact listening to your kids yourselves, there is hardly room for you and your children to grow into a mindful presence of conversational compatibility. Your kids will just grow-up fighting with each other, shouting over each other and not learning how to wait for a break in conversation for their turn to speak. When your child is slow, and they need to get something out in conversation, do you just override their moment, butt in yourselves and mute them then and there on the spot? If you do, or if their siblings do...or classmate, I can assure you that later on in life, the inability for them to feel open to speak in conversation will lower their self-esteem. As much as you may feel your child has little of importance to say about a subject, hearing them out at least for a few minutes, on their views, will increase their self-esteem tenfold in conversation. You as a parent, or teacher will get to know your child that much more. Should this not be priority?

➡ Great communicators are prepared and nurtured into well-spoken individuals from day dot. With reading and skilful conversations, learning the art of debate, your child can learn the art of having excellent communication skills. Most importantly, this should be something you practice with your child daily. Here are some strong points for you to follow and help you get started.

SWEARING AND FIRST INTRODUCTIONS

- As parents and teachers, we a know that great listening skills and how we come across to each other is a learnt behaviour. Some kids 'just get it' and some just don't. It takes time and continued repetitive effort to remind our kids when and when not to say something. Do you remember a time when you may have spoken to your partner about someone, or something, with your kids ears listening in on conversation, and you wish to this day that you never said it in front of them? Why? Well, because they repeated the exact same words to a new client of yours or a bit of gossip to the very friend you were gossiping about? What an embarrassment. As parents, knowing your own verbal boundaries in front of your children is extremely important. Or it may come back to haunt you.

- Avoid those swear words, your toddler or tween will be hearing them, thinking they are cool, and all grown up like their parents. I know well that when the schoolteachers hear those words, your kids may end up in the headmaster's office, and who's fault was it in the first place exactly? You as parents - your behaviour at home is what your children see. They were born with innocent brains, whatever is visually and auditorily put in front of them, they will see, copy, repeat.

- Introductions are an important bond between two people shaking hands. Here is the correct way you can teach your child the essential principals of introduction.

- Your children must always learn to use professional titles, such as Sir, Ma'am, Chief, President, Minister, Doctor... This shows a high regard of respect to the person or any 'pecking-order' which arises.

- Keep a metre of distance during introduction after shaking hands. We call this the 'safety zone rule'. No one wants to be practically stood on, or to be close enough in proximity to smell each other's breath.

- Use well fixed eye-contact and genuinely expressive facial expressions to show your enthusiasm in conversation and at meeting the person.

- Your kids can practice this with you at home and in a social setting in class or with friends.

- Avoid at all costs, trying to sound 'BIG' swearing mid-conversation. It does not show you in a good light and shows that you may have little well-mannered conversational skills.

- Five important keys:

- Stand tall and grounded.

- Smile.

- Make good eye-contact.

- Say your name.

- Shake hands.

BENEFITS OF SOCIAL SKILLS

→ Our children should have knowledge of basic social skills, which will not only enhance their self-esteem and confidence, it will improve their character and help them understand the importance of self-respect and respecting others. This provides your children with the fundamental tools we need in any given situation in today's day and age. This also gives them the foundation to build upon new and more mature complex social skills.

→ How we improve our children's brain development, speech and social interaction is by allowing them to focus on their inner qualities and behaviours, in any given situation or setting. Our children will then start to evaluate and create their own awareness of themselves and manage their behaviours with and around others.

→ We need to allow our children to grow and develop freely. Encouraging them from as young as three years old to use their mental capacity,' like a sponge soaking up liquid', and so your child will do the same, in whichever social setting you as parents, allow them to mentally and physically develop. As they say, 'you are your environment, and so you become', which also refers to the social group your children interact with. Encouraging our children to grow within a happy, loving, social and respectful environment, starting from home, is key.

WHAT ARE SOCIAL SKILLS?

ASKING THE BIG QUESTIONS

- Parents and teachers, here are some points to ask your children about social skills. Will they be able to come back with fruitful answers? Ask them to find out. I can guarantee they will say things that even you as adults will learn from. You can then follow on with each reply and create conversations regarding their views and emotions.

- Children, how can we encourage others? Can you all give me at least one example?

- Children, by taking turns to play with something, how does this show others how to behave?

- Children, if we are all to interact equally, why is this important?

- Children, when we are all sharing our games, books, and various other objects, how does this make you feel?

- Children, when we are all good listeners, what sort of atmosphere and interaction does this create for everyone?

- Children, when we are all speaking kindly about one another, using positive language, how does this make the other person feel? How does it make you feel?

- Children, do you treat others how you would like to be treated?

- Children, describe being a great role model, what does it entail? Are you a great role model?

- Children, are you kind and nice towards your peers? Be honest...

- Children, how do you feel about gossip and rumours?

- Children, if you were ever embarrassed by someone, how did it make you feel? Is it nice to be the person to embarrass someone else, as much as you may dislike them?

TEAMWORK & THE ART OF CONVERSATION

- Being open and encouraging with your child's communication skills, is the fundamental principle of allowing them to experiment as well as focusing on communication, whilst allowing our children to interact and express themselves. Building their knowledge, confidence, and self-esteem, with support they will progress to supporting their peer's mental growth, all whilst learning the art of kindness and sharing verbal cues. Some of your children will turn out to be the alpha role models in the group environment, we need them, it's the natural law of the universe to have a pecking order within a group setting. Most of the time it will just automatically happen naturally with children. They learn this pattern of behaviour from the day they were born. By working together as a collective team, your children will aspire and grow to be the well-rounded individuals society strives for, who share ideas, collectively converse with each other and congregate together to learn and inspire one another.

- Trying to teach our children to ask for help, or speak nicely to one another within the group environment, learning to manage their emotions with each introduction, is an art form they must all learn from a young age to master their self-esteem and confidence in every social setting possible. Not only that, how to treat everyone with the kindness and respect each of us deserve.

- Every person is different, not all situations or individuals can be treated in the same way, we all know this. By teaching your children from an early age how to manage each circumstance, without shouting or misunderstanding, is key to every situation. Managing emotions, taking a deep breath, speaking slowly and clearly with a managed tone of voice, is key to becoming a great conversationalist.

- Give your kids a scenario, practice these steps during the conversation.

RESOLVING CONFLICT

➡ Parents and teachers, conflict resolution is an especially important discussion to have with your children. Not only does it teach them how to behave in certain social settings, it also puts them in a 'good light'. Having a child who understands how to get themselves or their friends out of a sticky situation, is one of the most mature skills both adults and children can develop from an early age. Once they know how to do this, it will make not only your life easier, but especially theirs.

➡ Good conversation skills are not just about introductions, they are also about 'exit strategies' if things get too heated in discussion and how to ease one's way out of them.

➡ Here is a guided tour of what to teach your kids and how to manage their 'exit strategies' with their siblings and friends, without creating negative feelings. Life is all about strategizing and making transitions easy, especially with anyone we have emotionally invested ourselves with. So, things can get a little intense sometimes and we need to learn how to manage it.

➡ Solving conflicts is really understanding how we and how others feel. Sometimes our children will need to go directly to you as a parent, or teacher to discuss matters further.

➡ Sometimes removing ourselves from a heated argument quickly is the best way to deal with heated emotions. Take yourself off for a walk, read a book or delve into something creative.

➡ The next strategy for your child to do, is to think about the problem, then try to figure out a solution to the problem and thinking of alternatives. Not focusing on the problem, itself. There is a solution for everything.

➡ After the heated discussion and everything has calmed down, it may even take a few days, do apologise if you can, or open the conversation to do so. Even if it starts with a genuine message of some sort i.e. writing a sorry card, email, or letter. Don't try to make up over text. It never ends up well.

➡ Discuss the matter with the other person, listen to their view. Control your emotions. Resolve the conflict.

➡ Practice a scenario with your class or kids. Resolve the conflict with these exact steps.

➡ Conflict resolution is high on the list in creating effective communication skills early in life. Life is too short for hard feelings.

➡ Once you have practiced the scenario with your kids, ask them these questions, in this sequence:

➡ What caused the disagreement

➡ How does Jack feel? How does Oliver feel?

➡ Does anger make matters better or worse?

➡ In the end, does Jack or Oliver get what they wanted?

➡ Why is it important to resolve conflict peacefully or artfully? What happens if you can do so?

➡ What have you learned?

LOVING DISCIPLINE

➡ Parents, have you realised yet that how you discipline each one of your children, comes with a different 'kettle of fish'? Every child is different in personality, it is the hard reality that we are now in different times. Long gone are the days where any parent or headmaster is allowed to bring out the slipper or cane, and of course, if we did, it would be hugely frowned upon and we would more than likely end up in court. Our parents, and grandparents certainly had it differently to us in their day. I can also guarantee that most of them would say, "in my day we got the slipper, that's when discipline actually made kids listen. Through pain".

➡ Nowadays life has changed, there is no way in a million years any parent wants to get sent to prison over a slipper over their kids' rear ends. Sadly, though there is a lot of abuse which happens in homes, whether it be physical or emotional coercive control, it's there and it's not going away any time soon. As parents you would have been brought up in a household where you were taught discipline, in so many ways, and how your parents only used one strategy with you back then. Little did they know that there were far better disciplinary strategies out there which would have suited your character and psychology so much more. Which is what your own kids, would also do so much better if only you as a parent knew and did not bring old strategies of discipline into the equation like your parents did. Also, if you knew which form of discipline suited your child's character for them to grasp and let the punishment and lesson sink in so much quicker, they would learn so much more and still have kept high self-esteem.

DISCIPLINE

THE AGE RANGE

➡ Parents, one of the most intense parts of your lives as parents is when your babies become toddlers. It is a proven fact that the highest divorce rate happens when kids are toddlers. Can you imagine why? Suddenly you have tiny little people demanding your time and are struggling with your partner how to fix the tantrum toddler issue? Also, how to manage your own emotions having to deal with this issue for the first time ever. Having over 22 years working with families and disciplining their children, I would like to share some strategies with you in age format what is the best way to give your child that much needed disciplinary action. I can guarantee they will end up walking all over you otherwise.

➡ Respect that you are both in this together, but you don't necessarily always have to do the punishments together. The best strategies are sharing the stressful points, so you are both not jumping down each other's throats, after your toddler threw a tomato on the floor, or your tweens (which is a child becoming a teen, if you don't know what a tween is!) hormones are starting to kick in. Babies cry, we naturally can't stop this, so we will start with the toddlers, where it's either your life, or theirs and who is in charge!

HOW TO DISCIPLINE

THE TODDLER

- The feistiest being of all time, nothing overrides them if they can help it, they will test you no end. This is the one time in your life you will more than likely have the biggest 'fights' to win with your child, until they become a teen. But if you do this right, you lay down the rules early, your life will be so much easier.

- Depending on your child's character, you will tune in and work with them to give them a nurturing nudge on how to manage their emotions. Also, how to be strong with them, so that they know that no means no. In my experience, judging from the parents and the line of work they are in i.e. law, banking or corporate, their kids tend to be a lot more strong willed, it certainly is genetic. Toddlers are dealing with huge emotions, like frustration and anger. Male toddlers have more testosterone in them by the age of three than any other time in their lives. Can you imagine having to manage all this on your own at such an early age?

- A strategy for misbehaving at the table, turn the highchair away from the table facing away from everyone, at least half a metre away in case they try turning around to grab glasses, etc. This is if they have not listened a couple of times and it's the last resort. Don't practice this in a restaurant, do this at home so that once you are in a public space you can warn them - guaranteed they will stop immediately or face embarrassment in front of others.

- Hitting, kicking and being plain naughty. You may have no choice but to put them on the naughty step. This is better than a chair or object they can throw. As much as they scream, shout, and try to get up, keep gently placing them back there and walk away. If they are making themselves sick by getting worked up, then that is when you

220

take them off. Calm them down. Wait until they are totally calm, and then discuss why it was naughty and not to do it again. You must be strong. Do not leave them there for more than a few minutes at a time. Do not shout, you will do this in a silent and firm mode. Never hit the child in any way. Once the punishment is over and you ask if the child is ready to behave, allow them to get up and back to the group, or calm down through play or creativity.

➡ After an hour discuss the situation when they have calmed down. Use a soft tone and be kind. Try not to make them nervous. Make it a quick conversation, then say well done for listening and give them a star or sticker for good listening. Your partner must not be the one who the child runs to after the punishment, as the punisher you must see it out and create that bond again. Make it clear for your partner not to interfere until at least two hours after the tantrum, and then the hour of calm and discussion, also after the sticker. They can then go and show it off to your partner.

➡ Those cries can be excruciating on the ears, close the door behind you if you feel you can and it's safe for you to do so. SOME toddlers only learn by doing this strategy, with all the above. SOME toddlers absolutely will not work this way, they may be more sensitive, or their cognitive ability just cottons on to learning what is right and wrong quickly. It really all depends on the character of the child. If your child is strong willed, there may be only so much reinforcement one can do before they start becoming naughty and bored of it. That's when you know to stop, warn them where they will go if not careful. Two warnings are enough. Count to five. Usually by the number two they know to behave or else... You will be anchoring their minds back to a place they do not like being, that is enough to make any toddler feel uncomfortable. So, give them that count down chance after two warnings. They will test you, but you need to be firm. Poker face, even if you find them funny!

➡ Positive reinforcement is crucial along with the strategies above. They will want to behave better if you praise them for all the good things they are doing. Make sure you have stickers of their favourite animals or fairies etc, absolutely anything they do well, stick a sticker on them and say well done. If they misbehave, take one away. The aim is for you to give the stickers to them and for them to build self-esteem, so if you have to punish them, at least you know that they know that being good. Make sure that you have loads of stickers in your bag or pockets to stick on their clothes for excellent behaviour.

- If you are out in town, what if your toddler has a meltdown on the shop floor? Firstly, if you are experiencing 'the terrible two's' never go anywhere without a buggy. When the child has a tantrum, immediately strap them in the buggy and remove them from a crowded place. Never keep them in a venue or restaurant to ride out a tantrum. Immediately take them outside to calm down. Give distraction, show them a bird, a plane, or even a mobile phone to play on or iPad in the WORST CASE SCENARIO. Why stress yourself out, or even your own child? There is really no need.

- Usually tantrums will stop by 4 years old or sooner. Never try as a couple to both deal with it at the same time, only one partner should do this. The other should remove themselves, unless of course you don't trust your partners way of discipline. Best for you to do the tantrums if you are more patient than them. It is stressful, and even more so if your partner interferes. Keep things separate at this phase in your child's life with discipline.

- Check the time of day your toddler is having a tantrum. Is it late, are they hungry, do they have a temperature? Always have juice and snacks and a thermometer on you if you are out. These checks are also done at home. Keep to routines for nap times and meals. If there was ever a time where a routine is important, it is when your child is a toddler and spending copious amounts of energy on learning to walk, speak, and interact socially. This takes a huge amount of physical and mental power. Be mindful of this.

HOW TO DISCIPLINE YOUR CHILD

PART 1

➡ There are many ways to discipline the young child. Once they have grown from being a toddler into becoming a young child, hopefully by then they would have learnt a few valuable lessons. If you did the job well when they were a toddler, depending on your child's character and behaviour, guaranteed it will pave an easier pathway for you as they grow. SOME may agree with previous methods, some may not. Each family is different and how you punish your kids can be a very touchy subject for some. Fortunately, there are families who have had kids who have hardly ever had to be strong with their kids with discipline - incredibly lucky for them. Then there are parents who have had kids with behavioural problems so intense, that it has just taken over their lives in a big way. Was it the way they brought them up from toddlers, or is just the character of their child? Have they never known the real strategies which this child will learn from?

➡ Every child is different, how you punish one sibling may be completely the opposite to how you handle the other. With children as we know, structure is everything, it won't necessarily be as intense as it is with toddlers, there is a lot more flexibility and by now they should know right from wrong. Parents giving structure is the best discipline for children. This is how they learn, with structure and social interaction with others. Peer pressure kicks in and this is what you need to be aware of. This is the time you want to be careful who they are spending time together with, and who are their role models at school or at home. Structure is key throughout the day, with back to back social events and schooling, as well as set dates for playing with friends. Boys especially can be a bit wild with other boys around them, so be aware of this, and who they find exciting to be around and why.

HOW TO DISCIPLINE YOUR CHILD

PART 2

- A basic rule of thumb, this is where they will learn social skills and manners in a more formal school setting and etiquette through peer pressure. Discipline refers to preventing any future behavioural problems in the future.

- Kids need to learn appropriate behaviour in certain social settings. Whether it's at home, school or at a friend's house, they need to learn awareness to manage their own behaviour and feel comfortable at expressing their emotions.

- Try to remember the conflict resolution strategies in the pages before. This is how you, as a parent or teacher will manage a difficult child or situation. You must not ignore the fact that if you over discipline, this can crush your child's self-esteem, which lessens their confidence and growth. Too much negativity and not enough praise will rear a child with confidence issues and low self-esteem.

- Be fair but firm. Set limits and discuss the consequences of their actions if they act the same way again. Rewards and strategies don't change as they get older, you just need to think of rewards relevant to their age, either a movie, TV later on, playing on the game console, a play date, outing or the cinema. You can use these arrangements to take away from them if they don't behave. You are more flexible in your approach but still being firm with consequences in place if they behave badly. Spanking your children is not allowed in any shape or form. Of course, if you do this as a parent, be warned that later on in life there will be a tough teen to deal with if they have not been brought up with more intellectual ways of punishment.

- As a parent, you will need to be a good role model for behaviour, believe me, your kids are watching.

- Always praise your child for good behaviour, this is important with verbal praise when they are children growing into tweens.

- Set boundaries. You can do a 10 second count down after only the first warning at this stage, if they are really being naughty, stick to a shorter 5 second count down. They should not have the extra privilege of time. Warn of any consequences which may play out if they don't do something right or if they ever do the same thing again. You can, as a parent, and if you feel that the child is old enough or mature enough to take things on board with this heavy topic, discuss landing up in prison and what is involved, is not what they want.

- Manage your threats sensibly, not dressing fast enough is not a discussion for going to prison later in life, whereas stealing is.

- They should be past the naughty step strategy by 4 years old. The bedroom for timeout is often best, no electronics for the day or weekend, depending on severity of the punishment. Make them go read in their bedroom. Cancel a play date if seriously naughty, although this is not always good as it affects the other parents plans. As they get older you may ground them for a week, don't pay them their week's pocket money or take some money away. Speak to your friends with kids, guaranteed they will have strategies which also work.

- Bring in the conflict resolution strategies to manage the situation.

- Most importantly, once your child turns ten, or depending on their maturity close to that age, you must start nurturing them up into adulthood, not pushing their self-esteem down by keeping them mentally as children. They deserve a different approach from you, still with structure and firm consequences. Friendship and a close bond speak volumes going into their teenage years

- There will never be 'straight line' bringing up kids. You may have it good for a few weeks and then something else will happen which totally drives you crazy. The most important thing to keep calm in all situations. Your children will love you unconditionally, and at the same time test you to the limit. It is how you manage those moments and your approach to each different situation is what they learn from and are watching how you role-play it out. So be kind as much as possible, communicate. What feelings may they be experiencing because of something they have done or something that has happened to them. This is where your true parenting skills will be tested. As each child is so different in character, you as parents have the sole responsibility of knowing which approach to take which each given situation. Not all punishments suit all behaviours or outcomes. Be strategic, be firm be understanding of the situation before getting mad and make sure everyone knows they are loved and cared for after any form of discipline.

FAMILY HOLIDAY

PERFECT PACKING FOR HOT COUNTRIES

➡ After years of working with dignitaries, Royals, and professional corporate families, I have managed staff and children's suitcases extensively. Not only that, I have learnt from other staff what to take and what not to take in a suitcase, avoiding wasting space as well as making sure all the essentials are packed correctly for your kids holiday. I would like to offer you all my knowledge in this packing process, as I know things can be difficult when deciding what to take. I have seen families from foreign hot countries really confused on how to put their child into a snow suit and what their toddler should wear with it. I will give you step by step the guidance in what you should pack and how your children should put together clothes, from being respectful to different cultural practices, to combining clothes for various climates. Not only that, I will tell you in the next few pages, how to pack a suitcase. Most people will think they know already, which they don't. There is an art to this. Read on, this valuable information will set you up so that you are not lugging around truly large suitcases, as well as your own, for your kids and to save you ample amounts of space and time.

➡ For over 22 years working with high profile families, I have seen the very best of packing, as well as practicing my own packing techniques and living out of suitcases for months on end overseas. By the end of this, you will be so well rehearsed with not only packing your kids bags, but knowing the tricks to not have to even unpack or take up ample wardrobe space when you get to a hotel. You can leave the kids' clothes in their suitcases and use it as a cupboard, while you and your partner have all the cupboard space you want! I will start with what to pack for a toddler, and how much you need to take with you. Too often, I've seen parents over-pack clothes in suitcases which are never worn, then buying more clothes on holiday and not knowing where to put them on their return. Be strict with these packing strategies for toddlers and young children, you will be so pleased you did.

➡ During the process of packing, try not to ignore your kids if they want to help. You really should involve them. They must learn and understand the strategy and weight of packing a suitcase. Even your toddlers can carry some shoes, they love going to collect things from cupboards to bring them to you. Once you teach your kids about the art of packing early on in life, they won't be the ones with suitcases bursting at the seams looking clueless and not looking very well-travelled when they get to the airport. You know those people I'm talking about? The ones who have had to open their bags because of too much weight? Ok, we are ALL guilty of it at some point.

➡ Importantly, fixing this issue should start from now.

THE TODDLER AND CHILD

WHAT TO PACK FOR A HOT COUNTRY?
PART 1

➡ Firstly, you are going to buy the largest translucent sandwich zip bags you can find at the supermarket. Buy a few of them as you don't want to run out of them too quickly halfway through packing. Some of the largest bags are around 20 cm x 20 cm in size. If you can find bigger, then great. For a toddler's bag, that size is fine. You will use these bags for:

➡ Toiletries, medication, pants, socks, costumes, hairclips, hats, fun jewellery, crayons, sunglasses, bibs, grow-vests, tights, headphones and wires, vests, and shoes. Can you see where I'm going with this? These items will be packed totally separately from one another but packed neatly so that you can see through each translucent bag what is what. Not only that, these bags will 'snug' them together, so they don't all become loose and get mixed up. What you are creating is a 'cupboard' inside their suitcase. Or, you can take out each flat packed bag and place them in the cupboards, so that when it comes to repacking, all you will do is pick up those already flat packed bags, and be able to quickly re-pack, without having to fuss around with folding, etc.

➡ If you want to get more complex and organic, buy loads of white shoe bags online, then use a magic marker, (before you put any clothes inside them of course) and in capital letters, give each shoe bag a name. You can then draw-string them up for items to lie flat in the bags. Buy ones to fit sizes of toddler items, remember you want to keep things snug. Never throw these bags away when you buy new shoes, or after a holiday, keep them folded for your next holiday, including the sandwich bags used before. Start by making sure panties or underpants for your toddler are packed flat, on top of each other. Flat packing is key to start.

229

- ONE QUICK ONE FOR THE PARENTS. I hope you are still reading and not yet doing. Learn first this big tip, which is what I do. Buy the netted laundry bags, the ones with zips (to size of your shoes and clothes) then use those for snuggly putting away panties, bras, belts, etc. Parents, you can do this too. Transparent bags are great for shoes, trainers etc. If your stilettos or shoes of importance have a material bag, put them in a plastic translucent bag first, then slip them into the material bag after, so they have double protection and keep the material bags clean. If your shoes are too big, fit each shoe into one translucent bag at a time, then pair them up into the material bag.

- Netted laundry zip bags and shoe bags you can also to keep your toddler's shirts separated. Shorts and trousers, skirts, jackets, and jumpers separately as well. Not only does it keep their clothes hygienically clean, it keeps them tightly snug and flat packed to easily repack, then unpack when you get home. Why? Because all items will have its own home throughout the trip. You can also keep a separate laundry bag for clothes to be flat packed and washed on return, or, taking the bag to the local laundry on holiday, in your villa, or leaving it for your hotel to wash and re-deliver to your hotel room. So, buy one large netted zip laundry bag for you to have at hand when travelling. They are light and easy to move around and you will be able to flat pack them easily in your suitcase. Then pop them into a tote bag when walking through town without laundry spilling out of your bag.

- OK, BACK TO YOUR TODDLERS. Socks fold once, Vests only one-fold in half. Costumes fold once and don't bundle, keeping one-fold for everything is key! Hats lay flat, one on top of each other. Shoes are packed individually in pairs, only one translucent bag at a time, this will keep the inside of the bag clean. After each use, place them back inside the bags in the suitcase, until the next use. The plastic sandwich bags are really a must for shoes. Material shoe bags are best for underwear, vests, hats, and costumes. Anything messy i.e. crayons, magic markers etc translucent bags are best for anything that may leak.

➡ Before you get started, this strategy is important. The main compartment of the suitcase is only to be used for clothes. The side of the suitcase with an elastic tie, you will use for medications and all the above mentioned i.e. shoes, pants, socks, vests, wires, all the essential extras, hairclips and toiletries.

➡ PLEASE CARRY ON READING BEFORE YOU START

THE TODDLER AND CHILD

WHAT TO PACK FOR A HOT COUNTRY?
PART 2

➡ In this section, I am going to tell you what to take and how much to take. Remember that you are a busy parent, you have only so much time to spend on packing, you have to be strategic and think about the holiday, weight of items and dress code for the country. Also, the heat.

➡ Some of you may find this hard to get your heads around. What if I were to tell you this? Let's say you are going away for three weeks and I said to you, please whatever you do, do not pack for three weeks. Only pack for one week. Why? Well because that is all your toddler needs. Are you going to not wash their items for three weeks? I don't think so. You will wash them frequently. So, from now on, you will pack for only one week for a toddler, with a few extra items for accidents. No more than that. You will also do this with your older kids. And for yourselves once you know the strategy.

➡ What to take to a hot country for your male toddler:

➡ Why do you only pack for a week? The idea and proven method is so that you do the laundry when you are away, you will not run out of clothes if you keep on top of it. If clothes are clean after a day's use, you can recycle them to be worn the next day. Or you can give them a quick wash every evening on a quick 15-minute cycle, depending on stains. Are you staying in a villa? If so, then super. Hotels will charge you less than being overweight at the airport luggage check-in counter.

➡ X2 hats

➡ X2 costumes

232

- X7 bibs

- X10 grow-vests (sleeveless)

- X10 pairs of underpants if they are out of nappies

- X7 shorts

- X7 shirts

- X3 sets of pyjamas (with long sleeves for air-conditioned rooms)

- X10 pairs of socks

- X3 smart trousers for the evenings

- X3 long sleeved light jumpers for the evenings

- X3 cotton long sleeved button up or closed light weight tops for the evenings

- X1 set of slippers

- X1 pair of trainers

- X1 pair sandals for the beach

- X1 pair smart shoes for evening outings

A TODDLER AND CHILD

WHAT TO PACK FOR A HOT COUNTRY?
PART 3

- For your little female toddler, what will you take to master one weeks' worth of packing for a hot country? Some countries which have strict rules on female dress codes, still refers to young girls. So, you must abide by their rules on how much skin can be exposed. Light cotton outfits which are flowing are best below the knee for certain countries. Little girls tend to get away with taking more on holiday for dress codes. That is ok but keep it minimal.

- X10 pairs of ankle or trainer socks

- X10 panties (If they are potty trained and out of nappies)

- X10 grow-vests or just vests if they are using them rather than grow-vests. (Sleeveless)

- X7 T-shirts

- X5 pairs of shorts (If you prefer that she wears dresses, take 5 dresses and only two pairs of shorts)

- X2 skirts

- X2 pairs of thin tight flexible wearing trousers, or loose (whichever she prefers wearing)

- X3 light long sleeved tops

- X3 dresses for day wear

- X2 dresses for evening wear (keep them knee length)

- X3 sets of pyjamas (with long sleeves, for air-conditioned rooms)

- X2 light jerseys or jumpers for the evening

- X1 mix and match light coloured smart button-up jumper for the evening, if going out.

- X10 bibs

YOUR KID'S HOLIDAY IN THE SUN

PART 1

➡ Now that you have placed all your toddler's clothes on the bed, proceed to start packing their suitcase. If you do this right, you can fit it all in perfectly well with ample space to bring back bought items on return. Don't feel you need to keep filling up the gaps, this is a huge mistake and it will cost you.

➡ For your child's suitcase, a medium size suitcase is big enough, I have seen cabin size suitcases being used as well, if you are savvy enough! You can also fit their items into your own suitcase if you also stick to the one-week method of packing. If you have two or more children, depending on age range, you can still create this perfect strategy with ease for a seven-day packing strategy for each child.

➡ Never roll the clothes. This is an old strategy and takes up way more space than you think. You are going to flat pack absolutely all their clothes. Use the side of the suitcase which has the zip-up pullover netting. That side is for the clothes. Start by unfolding the clothes and laying them all inside one by one, dresses, trousers, jumpers, and shorts. Only fold the trousers once at the knee if you must. Fold the jumper long arms in, only once along the front of the chest, for each item.

➡ You will use your snug netting bags, shoe bags and translucent bags for all other items to flat pack on top of those items already packed in the zip-up side, which are easy to take out and put back in again, keeping things neat and tidy as you go along.

➡ Best you choose the clothes for the kids each day, this way you can keep on top of neatness for when it comes to packing. Or always train the kids about the importance of keeping these bags flat packed and neat. Of course, with your toddler, it's better you choose their clothes daily.

➡ Shoes should be packed sole to sole on their sides, in translucent bags on the clip side of the bag, along with medications, toiletries, crayons, nappies, etc, which will all be in their own separate bags, as previously mentioned. These will be easy to take out of the suitcase and put into a cupboard, then re-pack once you leave. You just pick it up, pack and go. Any new clothes can be flat packed in the zip-up side of the bag, where you left space to do so.

➡ Make sure anything heavy is put at the bottom of the suitcase, so when you turn it up right, you are not squashing items of clothing. Toiletries are best for this; summer shoes can go at the top where they are light and easy.

➡ When you arrive at your destination, there will be no need to hang up any items or take any items out of the suitcase which already has a bag as a home. Only dresses or jackets will need to be hung up if necessary. You can keep the bag open as a cupboard, and just close it in the day when you go out, keeping items safe.

YOUR KIDS' HOLIDAY IN THE SUN

PART 2

THE BIG TIPS ARE:

- You will do the exact same strategy for your young children, minus the nappies, bibs, and grow-vests. So, as they thankfully get older, there is less to take!

- FOR THE AEROPLANE - Preparation and easy travelling is key. Gone are the days where you dress up for a flight, nowadays people understand that going through security and check-in, is all about strategizing, comfort, and style. These are the big tips, so you are not fussing with your kids as you try take them through the most stressful part of the journey.

- Make sure they are wearing slip-on shoes and a warm, soft woollen beany hat and a fleece for the duration of the journey. Long well fitted socks to prevent DVT (deep vein thrombosis) from altitude.

- They should wear tights or jeans, nothing with a belt, loose hanging tops and t-shirts.

- No jewellery at all, keep the minimal amount in your bag, if you need to put it on, do it on the other side.

- Keep any electronics all together in one bag, so you can take it out all together and your kids are not shuffling about.

- They can each take one small backpack, for crayons, X3 slim books, X2 colouring in books. Also, headphones if your kids need them for take-off. They will have a lot of movies to get through.

- Make sure to buy that extra bottle of water each once through check-in for the plane.

- Take hand sanitizer and make sure you use it all the time

- Each child must have a spare pair of pjs and slippers. Nappies for the duration of the journey and spare set of clothes just in case, depending on the age of your kids. Toothbrush and toothpaste are a necessity. You can also have a facecloth per person in a plastic bag to freshen up. Take two plastic bags, one for dirty cloths. Nappy bags and all those essential items go in your nappy bag. Thermometer, allergy medication and wet wipes can go there too.

- Passports and visas should all stay with you. If you manage, you can fit this into just one cabin bag. Make sure it has four wheels, not two. This is much easier to handle when it comes to kids.

- Make sure to take their favourite blanket or sleeper toy on the journey, they can also use their noise cancelling earphones to cover their ears for naps. Have some jelly babies or something similar for them to chew on to help with popping ears and altitude.

- Toys – Generally speaking, no more than a shoe box full of light weight toys can be packed sensibly in their large suitcases. 7 small toys maximum.

- Make sure that you are dressed appropriately with the correct clothes for your destination, and so are your kids.

- When on holiday and going into a big cultural city of certain social settings and religion, your children must be dressed appropriately. Don't think that because they are children, they can get away with an irresponsible dress code in strict countries. Be respectful and mindful of your appearance at ALL times.

PACKING PERFECTLY FOR THE SNOW

YOUR KID'S WINTER HOLIDAY

- Again, we will start sensibly with your toddlers. Young children will take all the below as well and you will pack their suitcases in the exact same way as you did for the summer holiday, but with warm clothes. Of course, there is less space with larger coats, etc, which you will need to be mindful of. Again, you will pack for only one week. 7 days. You will be surprised how a lot of families from foreign hot countries find it tricky to know what to pack, or how to put their toddler's snowsuit on. There is more to packing with the complexities of colder countries. Not only that, you need to think carefully on the seasons and what to take. Let us first start with the male toddler.

- Let's say they are going for a skiing holiday, we will cover the important outfits and you can take them out if they are not going to a snowy country, but where it is still cold and wet. This outline will also refer to your older kids, minus nappies, bibs, etc.

PACKING PERFECTLY FOR THE SNOW

YOUR KIDS WINTER HOLIDAY

- WHAT YOUR KIDS MUST WEAR FOR A SNOWY COUNTRY. GENERALLY, THEY WILL WEAR THE SAME CLOTHING, ADAPTED FOR TODDLERS AND YOUNG CHILDREN.

- X10 bibs

- X10 underwear (If potty trained)

- X10 grow-suits (short sleeved, not sleeveless)

- X5 thermal long tights & X5 thermal long-sleeved tops. (Sets. If you buy onesies in thermal wear, I wish you good luck in getting them on and off while changing nappies!) Tuck the tops into the thermal bottoms, after you put a grow-vest on the toddler. Children can just wear a short-sleeved vest under the thermal wear, depending on how cold it is. Layering is key to keeping warm.

- The best time to put on a snow suit is after your toddler has done their morning 'number 2'! A snow suit is super tricky to take off if you don't. Just to warn you and save you time.

- X10 pairs of over the ankle, calf socks. Always put socks on first, so to tuck under the thermal bottoms when you slide the thermal bottoms on.

- X5 long sleeved shirts, stretchable, with high neck. Tuck shirt into thermal bottoms.

- X4 long sleeved stretchable shirts, With holes for thumbs for older kids. Without high necks. Tuck shirt into thermal bottoms.

- X3 lightweight zip-up fleece or jumpers. Use a thin fleece over a stretchable shirt for an extra layer of warmth.

- X2 neck warmers for snowy weather. Make sure to put this on after the fleece.

- X2 scarves. Wrap the scarf around your kids' neck before getting into the snowsuit.

- X2 pairs snow gloves. Make sure to put these on after putting on the fleece or jumper, and before your kids slip into the snowsuit.

- X2 woollen winter-warm beanies, worn at all times outdoors.

- X2 snow suits, 100% waterproof, which have room for movability and play. You will put the snow suits over the clothes mentioned above. You do not put trousers on over thermals to go in a snow suit, ever. It will be too hot.

- Snow boots go on last. Make sure you only put a snow suit on the very last minute you are about to go out into the snow. They can get hot to wear if not careful. Have water on you, wherever you go. Snow boots go under the snowsuit at the ankles.

- For older kids, you can get the snow suits which have braces, they will go over all layers of clothes.

- Older kids will wear a waterproof, hooded coat, worn last after all clothes have been layered on, including gloves. Make sure to put them on before the coat. If the snow suit is thin for your toddler, they must also wear a waterproof jacket. Everything must be 100% waterproof, avoid synthetic materials.

- Indoors they will just wear their thermals after being outside to play, and indoor slippers

KIDS PACKING PERFECTLY FOR THE COLD WINTER

➡ This list will cover what is needed for all your kids ages, take out the obvious and add the obvious, depending on your child's age.

➡ X2 Beanies

➡ X2 Warm scarves

➡ X2 Sets of warm finger gloves

➡ X5 Sets Grow-vests or short sleeved vests, X2 long sleeved

➡ X1 Warm winter jacket which is colour coordinated for all outfits. Preferably a coat thigh length for girls. (Thick duck feather is ideal)

➡ X5 Thermal wear sets, long tops, long bottoms.

➡ X3 Pairs, long sleeved pyjamas

➡ X5 Pairs of trousers

➡ X5 Long sleeved shirts

➡ X3 high neck long sleeved shirts

➡ X1 pair of hard-wearing boots

➡ X1 pair trainers

➡ X1 pair of slippers

➡ X3 Sets of jumpers or Woollen cardigans

➡ For girls, you can take X3 Winter daytime dresses

➡ X2 Pretty evening dresses matched with winter tights and matching cardigan

➡ X5 pairs of tights to wear under dresses or skirts. Mix and matched to outfits

➡ X1 Set of long boots for girls

➡ X1 pair of closed shoes to wear over tights

➡ X1 pair of slippers

KIDS PACKING PERFECTLY FOR SPRING AND AUTUMN

- Both seasons in cold countries are easy to dress for. Your children can wear the same thing during these seasons. They won't be as layered as the winter seasons, which is straight forward and easy. One thing to remember though, never leave the house in any cold country without an umbrella. The same applies for the winter months. Even if you think it looks sunny, the weather can change in seconds, be ready to get warm and cover yourself if the rain falls out the sky.

- X1 light-weight jacket, preferably a very thin layer of padding or light duck feather is ideal. Not heavy duck feather or padding as you would in winter. You will use this for the colder breezy days.

- For a hotter day, a light-weight waterproof parka is enough. Make sure it goes to mid-thigh for girls. Boys can wear a coat to the waist.

- Under the light-weight coats, the kids will take and choose to wear from...

- X2 cotton scarves, mixed and matched

- X10 pairs of thin socks

- X10 underwear/panties

- X2 light-weight beanies, not heavy wool, thin wool

- X7 vests or grow-vests, with short sleeves

- X7 pairs light weight trousers

- X5 long sleeved tops

- X3 T-shirts

- X2 pairs shorts for boys

- X4 long sleeved jumpers and cardigans, mixed and matched to outfits
- X2 skirts with mix and match tights for girls
- X3 daytime dresses for girls, mixed and matched with light weight tights
- X2 evening dresses for girls with mix and match evening woollen tights
- X1 pair of slippers
- X1 pair of flat ankle boots
- X1 pair trainers
- X1 pair of closed evening shoes for the boys and girls
- Lastly, structure your holidays before you go to keep the peace, and to also have time as a parent to do your own thing. HAPPY HOLIDAYS!

STRUCTURED PARENTING

STEAL BACK VALUABLE TIME

PART 1

● PARENTS- Too often we seem to think that giving our child/ children more of our time is exactly what your kids need. In some circumstances, yes certainly, but not all the time. Children are extremely adaptable beings, far more resilient than you or I, as we grow into adulthood. What you teach your child early on in life, is what they will become. What they see and hear when a tiny baby, is like a sponge soaking up liquid. How you adapt to their general well-being as well as their daily routine, is exactly what they will learn. How you manage their routine, as well as your own routine combined is what they will learn to absorb and 'know'. So, to cut a long story short, however you manage your kids and your own life, will give you freedom to create an 'adoptive' behaviour from your own kids. It will be what they grow up with, and not really know any different, until they are old enough to compare. By that time, your children will probably be teenagers, ready to take on the world, who may have been brought up by you as well rounded individuals in society, or resentful beings instead. That is a fact of life, and we all know, at some point in our lives, we became resentful of something our parents did, whilst we were in our prime years growing-up. Hardest hit are those children who never had parents at all and had to learn to adapt into a new family, or just fight for survival on their own.

● Luckily though, there are a lot of wonderful parents out there, who are well bonded and well-grounded families, looking out for only the absolute best for their children. Some parents are adaptable to their children's needs, some parents are not. Some parents leave the parenting up to their hired nannies or carers and don't want to do the

really hard stuff. That's ok, because like I say, children are adaptable and social beings. We expect this from life. This does not mean that parents don't love and care for their kids. It just means there are so many aspects to not being around your own children all day, from working in jobs and supporting your income to your kids' education, to those parents who are focused on setting their own boundaries, even if they are stay at home parents, who outsource well educated nannies etc to help out at home.

STRUCTURED PARENTING

STEAL BACK VALUABLE TIME
PART 2

➡ The long and short of this is, are you as parents, managing to create enough structure to steal back your time? And I don't mean just going to work, your kids are at school and that is fine. I'm taking about, the time you have with you. Yes, yourself. The time you spend freely with your partner. The time where you go on a quick three day break away from your kids? Are you the type of parent where you would not dream of leaving your kids with another person and find your own over controlling behaviour will never allow you to win at conquering all the above? These are questions you really should start asking yourself. How will you cope later in life when your kids start flying the nest? Would you have given them the opportunity of independence growing up, which would help them fly comfortably from that nest, into the greater wilder world?

➡ The point which is being made here is this. Without 'letting go of your child' and allowing them to experiment as well as 'independently grow' when they are younger, and adapting to your absence, you will make them more and more reliant on you as they get older. Guaranteed it will take them longer to leave the 'over nurtured, staying at home with the parents all the time nest' you subjected them to. And despite all this time and effort in doing so, where did your valuable time go? To do all the wonderful things life offers you? Or focusing on the talents you were born with? To smother your kids not only decreases your children's ability to develop their independence, it also creates a suppressive environment for them, or for you to steal back your precious time.

■ Parenting is about 'give and take' with your kids, which they should learn from an early age. Without structure or routine in your day, you will never have time to do the things you really enjoy. By giving your child a day full of structured events, from sports clubs, playdates, allowing other adults to also give them the best of their abilities, how else will they learn flexibly from others? All this leads to their development.

■ PARENTS, guaranteed, you will never know everything, not even your kids will feel they learned everything from you growing up. This is exactly what good parenting is, adapting your child to other people and their teachings. Allowing them to grow and flourish, meeting all their various sensory and socially interactive needs, in every way possible, within the confines of love, guidance, and the right peer groups. Sharing your children with those close to you, who adore having your children around, granting you with a 3 day break, while you head off to Paris with your partner. Have you thought about how others may wish to have what you have, sharing your kids for a few days could change their world for the better? So it is time parents, feel less guilty, allow your children the gift of independence, being around and learning from others, let go and give yourself and your children the gift of time, without you controlling their every move. The more structure in your day, the more life you both will have. Not only will your mental health improve, it will also enhance your quality of life,

STRUCTURED PARENTING

MANAGING ELECTRONICS

PART 1

➡ Life has changed dramatically over the years, long gone are the days of not having technology or social media at hand. If anything, life has become a lot easier for parents in so many ways, if not, harder as well. How do we strip our kids off the iPad, or their gaming consoles, without actually having a plan for the children to do afterwards, or is it just a feeling of guilt that you gave them too much time on it in the first place? Is it really their fault? Parents are having to adapt more than ever, schools are now demanding that children learn more from sitting on the internet and generally speaking, it is taking away valuable one-to-one time with real people, which is making our children scarily addicted to watching screens all day. Mental health is something we need to sort out right now, all those guilty feelings as a parent, knowing full well that just handing over the iPad will solve many problems like tantrums, sibling rivalry or passing time on a long journey.

➡ Where has all the valuable time gone if us as adults use those precious moments, which you actually do have with your kids, focused on electronics instead? How do you structure your child's day, so that you know there is a specific time to play games on the internet, only after they have read books, played puzzles, done their homework, helped putting away the dishes, showered, had dinner etc and so it goes on. Have you, as a parent, given up and got to the point of, well it's just so much easier if I do this on my own, I know the iPad will entertain them while I do this. Sadly, society (parents) has become increasingly reliant on this strategy. Well, is it the wrong, or right strategy? You tell me.

➡ Personally, I find it a lazy one, a strategy which is not really a strategy for them, more a strategy for you, to ease your struggle with daily structures and tiredness. We 'get it', it is understandable, to a point. But how do we get rid of this? I say this to all parents, without making a fuss - you can fix this issue, you just have to know how to do it properly, which will make your children learn with, structured positive reinforcement and rewards, rather than using it for your own emotional needs, and gain with time control at home. Is this making you feel guilty? That you have lost invaluable time already with your kids glued to their tech?

STRUCTURED PARENTING

MANAGING ELECTRONICS
PART 2

- Kids love to have structure; they also learn best through a structured environment and structured parenting. This is where you come in. If you allow your kids to play on their iPads all day, when will they learn flexibly at home from creating puzzles, reading, arts and crafts and so on? When will you have time to show them how to learn from your own talents as a parent?

- Kids should be rewarded for good structure at home, where you give then at least a chore a day to do, along with the outline of a normal daily routine.

- Children should be allowed to have the 'space' in their environment and minds each day where you actually say to them "go do whatever you would like to do for the next hour, except for anything electronic or TV". This allows their mental development to get creative within their surroundings. As humans, we learn from an early age to adapt and be creative within our environment with freedom of choice. That is how we develop and grow. How will you learn, or how will your child learn to develop their natural born talents if they are sitting on electronics all day? Will our talents even exist so much if our kid's mental capacity to grow and flourish is tempered, if technology has taken over their lives. Parents need to give boundaries and structure at home?

- You will see increasingly our kids' talents are being taken over from social media. This, we need to be aware of, and it's time as parents to take control and not allow social media or electronics to take away or structured home settings, kids talents that they can be proud of.

➡ This must stop. It is up to parents to do what is important. Create structure at home, make sure your children are learning from you and how to run a home. Reward and encourage them with positive reinforcement as much as possible, rather than just telling them to stop. Could this be the reason why they find more solace with staring at a screen these days? Ask yourself that question.

STRUCTURED PARENTING

THE POWER OF TRANSITIONS
PART 1

➡ PARENTS, teachers - transitions...in all my years working with children from various learning abilities, and without actually having the understanding of the importance of transitions, sometimes I thought that I would just never make it through. Whatever that might be, it's more a general speaking of how this child will remain calm, how will I remain calm if I'm not patient enough to create the perfect transition. Transitioning is everything, guaranteed. If you as a parent have learnt the art of transitioning with your children, everything else will become an absolute breeze.

➡ Having worked with children of all abilities, ages, capabilities and eclectic characteristics, there are a few wonderful transitioning methods which work like a dream. With every transition, there come emotions. Emotional pulls of all kinds, from sadness to happiness, to anxiety and pain. How we manage these emotions in our children is everything to make your lives and their lives so much happier. If you are too overbearing in a transition, this can cause frustration in your child, like smothering them when they just want you to disappear quickly. On the other hand, if you are too quick to cut them off, this can create deep anxiety which can make your child become anxious in the long term, learning behaviours of rejection. This is where you, as a parent, must learn the 'fine-line' of transitioning, where your children can feel comfortable within the 'confines' of 'flexibility' guided through the carefully constructed transition. Does this make sense? I hope so.

➡ The transition in every situation must be given with love, nurturing and care. But also, with being mindful to your child's age and their peer group. As they get older, it's not really about you as a parent, where you feel hurt if they don't want to hang out with you. In most cases, it's more that they have grown independent enough to feel more comfortable being away from you and building their own lives. Those great transitions you did all along allowed them to feel comfortable enough, with enough flexibility, to come and go with ease, and to grow independently into their own lives with self-assurance and confidence. Which is what 'letting go of your child and allowing them to grow' means.

STRUCTURED PARENTING

THE POWER OF TRANSITIONS
PART 2

- Always be kind and use a soft tone during a transition.

- Be flexible on arrival and flexible with your approach on exit, when arriving at a destination, to hand over your child.

- Keep the situation 'calm and collected'. Encourage a toddler to get stuck into something mentally first.

- Be consistent with times, you and the children can manage with clocks and watches. Make sure you also have a gentle discussion with them that not all the time arrival or departures are exactly 'on the clock', even though time management is important.

- Explain to your children why time management is important. Not only does it not waste their time, it also keeps everyone's time schedules working well for appointments, playdates etc.

- Discuss this with your older kids -time and transitions are not just about that particular time. The events and times leading up to that time, as well as after, are just as important. During the day there is a schedule, there is a structure to why we do things and for good reason. What are those reasons? Ask your kids to 'think out of the box' and answer you.

- You can use the countdown strategy of 5-10 seconds or give more time if they are feeling frustrated. There is no reason for you as a parent to get yourself stressed, or your child stressed, if there is really no need to be in a hurry to get anywhere. The countdown always works like magic, starting from saying 10 minutes left, planting a 10-minute seed in their minds, or 5 minutes if you are running late.

Going down to saying 5 minutes left, if you started from 10 minutes (which is often the best strategy). Then saying 2 minutes left. By then, they have subconsciously put their own minds into perspective and may have built up their own strategy to put the project to one side until they can find time to come back to it. Always say the last 2 minutes on a countdown. It will make your kids think quickly after having the first 8 minutes to finish off what they were doing, which may have been important to them.

- By 2 minutes, this is when you say to them to get ready and time to put on their shoes and coats, etc. Always start this process half an hour before you go. This really is up to you as a parent to not stress the transition with poor time keeping.

- Alarm clocks can be useful. Give a 15-minute countdown, knowing you have a full half hour for them to get ready. You will set the alarm clock and tell the kids that in 10 minutes time, when the alarm goes off everyone must get ready. They will only then have 5 minutes to get ready. That way, it is their own pressure of time pushing them, not you nagging. Try it. Each child is different, so it may work better where they can think for themselves independently. You may get a surprise seeing them sitting there waiting for you.

- Sometimes creating a strategy in game form with alarm sounds, or who's going to win, is actually also quite fun for the little ones. Or "quickly, did you see the rabbit, or mouse? Quickly, let's put your shoes and coat on to look for where it ran." It's all about creativity and making the transition easy with imaginary games.

- Imagine your boss came into your office, demanding that you get up and go right away? Not even having time to close your open emails, and computer? Wouldn't that 10 minutes warning have been important to transition your day properly?

- Transitions are EVERYTHING to keeping your lives easier, without a fight with your kids, but also teaching them better skills and keeping their mental health at ease.

SET MEAL PLANNING

SAVING MONEY & TIME
PART 1

➡ Shocking isn't it? Going to the super market and you see a mum with three kids in tow running behind the trolley, often crying for something she's said "no" to, trolley piled high with absolute junk food? And there you are, trying to focus on your shopping list, or your elderly mother is with you with all the noise and screaming kids breaking the sound barrier. Don't even get me started!

➡ So, what exactly are they feeding their kids? You ask yourself; do they have a strategic plan? Or nothing at all in place, which would keep them sane and save cash. Are we ALL guilty of this same sort of episode as parents at some stage? Erm...absolutely. So best we don't point fingers and try to be mindful,

➡ We all know how hard it can be as parents feeding your kids, worrying about the next pay check coming in, knowing that even though you are not feeding your kids so well, at least they are being fed. Really though, is this the right approach? Certainly not, and there is a perfect strategy to get through the tough times, and the times when it's not so hard for you. Ideally, if you have an awesome structure in place which ticks all the boxes, you won't regret it. If you stick to this strategy, you won't be the mum who seems a totally disorganised mess, with your children running riot in the shops, which all parents have had to subject themselves to. Of course, thankfully as mums and dads, overriding such circumstances at your local supermarket is totally forgiven, we are all in this together to overcome looking a bit of a mess and not getting it perfectly right all the time.

➡ We shall start by strategizing a perfect weekly meal plan and how to do it. It's simple and basic, without going into recipes and particular meals. Follow the strategy to feed your kids with skilled planning, prior planning, and thoughtful action. I promise, this will make your life so much easier, with less food waste and more saved cash in the bank. Your kids will also understand the importance of meal planning, little waste, and structured daily meals and a well thought out weekly menu.

SET MEAL PLANNING

SAVING MONEY & TIME
PART 2

- TRIED, PROVEN, TESTED AND SENSIBLE. Start by discussing with your children what their favourite meals are. Sit down with them and go through a super list of meals which you know they love already. Give them options throughout your long list of meals, as well as a few new interesting things to try, let them know you will be trying out a new food every week and everyone will see how they go. They are surely going to say, we love chocolate cake, ice-cream, french fries, etc, which is why you will need to create the list first and ask them, what they particularly like best out of that list of NUTRITIOUS meals you have on offer. Make it easy for them and yourself by creating a 3-food strategy for every dinner plate, which will be a vegetable, meat, and carbohydrate i.e. potatoes, risotto, pasta etc. For now, you are only going to focus on the dinner time meal planning for the week.

- Setup a Monday – Sunday list for dinners, every night is now sorted. You know what to buy. Write a separate list for ingredients.

- Your kids and you have now created a plan of delicious dinners for the week. Done.

- Every week, you will only go buy fresh food from your list. If the kids don't like something, cross it off during the week and replace it with something new. Keep pen and pad magnetised to your fridge door.

- Go online, there are amazing recipes for kids, which you can try to cook for them weekly. It's all about strategizing and getting creative.

- Every week, try introducing two new meals, spaced apart, for the kids to try. Replacing them with the old meals, or meals not previously liked. Space them apart so that at least you don't have two new meals they don't like together, two days in a row.

- By doing this, you will save a lot of money rather than doing a huge shop, with a lot going to waste by the end of the week.

- The reason for not looking so much into lunch time meals is because you will more than likely be using leftovers from the night before to finish off the next day. You can strategically make a little extra for the next day.

- For lunchtime (holiday meals) you will also make a list for 7 days. Will it cover bread to make simple sandwiches with various meats and cherry tomatoes, cheeses, yoghurt etc? Lunch time meals do not need to be large. Guaranteed, you will be able to eat leftovers the next day from a lasagne from the night before. So, buy light food for lunches for kids.

- For breakfast, think of what the kids love to eat, other than sugary cereals. Can you make homemade sugar free muffins for the week? Or buy a dozen eggs, which will be an egg and toast during the mornings, with chopped cucumber? This is all about money saving and healthy eating. If you can find exactly what your kids love to eat, are able to divide the food perfectly for each day with real measurements per head, you will make wonderful breakthroughs.

SET MEAL PLANNING

SAVING MONEY & TIME

PART 2

➡ A BIG TIP. Purchase all your heavy-to-carry tins, water bottles, pastas, rice, and any form of dry goods online, which will last you for the whole month at least. So, you go online at the beginning of each month and purchase what you feel will cover a months' worth of dry goods you use in the house. Include detergents, soaps, chemicals for cleaning etc. Yes, you may have a few £ or $ delivery charge, but that's ok, it's not like you are doing it every week, and I can assure you, it will be the best thing you did rather than lugging loads if items around in store. Not only that, you can get great deals online from just looking at the comparisons from the sofa or in your office. You will be pleased you did this, trust me! Choose an evening slot when the kids are in bed, or daytime slot, when the kids are at school. We are in the 21st century and have the luxury of doing this. When you have kids, it's worth every penny - and your precious time. When all the dry goods arrive, pop your gloves on, you can use throwaway disinfectant wipes and wipe it all down before putting items away. Or just use a cloth and Dettol spray.

➡ Each week, you will now go and purchase any fresh foods in-store on your meal plan. Buying fresh foods online is not great, you just don't know what you are going to get when it comes to meat, dairy and vegetables. Plus, there is the worry of E. coli, so it's best you purchase these items in-store. This is all about planning, money saving, strategizing, and eating fresh for each week. You will know by now the exact veg to buy, without going off on a tangent. Any dry ingredients for each meal plan, you should have bought online at the beginning of the month. If the ingredients are not online, you can buy them at the same time as your fresh foods.

- Plan to shop when the kids are at school or go first thing in the morning if you are a busy parent. Or share childcare duties to do your fresh food shopping meal plan later in the evening. Childcare can be an issue; we all know this. Therefore, to make life simpler, it's is easier to do things this way and it's also much quicker.

- If you are looking to do something less expensive than a supermarket, go to your local open-air market for vegetables. Guaranteed you will find fruit and vegetables for half the price than your local average supermarket, and maybe some other exotic fruits for them to try. Personally, I still prefer to buy my meats from a good supermarket, where my meat has been well packaged, and I know that it's organic and not battery farmed. Buying free range or organic meats, eggs and dairy is important. Understandably though, some don't for financial reasons, and we need to be mindful of this. If you think about it though, if you buy cheaper vegetables and fruit at the local market, along with your monthly dry goods shop, where you can compare deals online automatically, you can actually carry out an organic meat, dairy and eggs shop for great fresh weekly ingredients. Plus, you won't be spending cash on unnecessary junk food.

SET MEAL PLANNING

SAVING MONEY & TIME
PART 3

➡ A BIG TIP- At the end of each month have a FREEZER WEEK. Use up all your left-over frozen foods or boxed frozen foods. Kids often LOVE freezer week, especially if you have hidden fish fingers and ice cream floating around in the back somewhere. Too often parents will put things away in their freezers (for when World War 3 breaks out...) and never use these foods. Why are we still doing this and using this sort of behaviour when life is so different now? So, go on, save money, save time, save space, check your freezer, or buy a good box freezer for FREEZER WEEK. Pull out what has been hidden in the back there for months on end and create space for the new meals your kids are learning to love with new eclectic and acquired tastes.

➡ Choose two days a week for dessert. Which days are they allowed? Are you sure you want to do this and not have moody kids the next day? What is their choice of dessert? A yoghurt with less sugar? Rice pudding? How are you going to choose a 'dessert like food' for after dinner? Are they allowed just a yoghurt after each evening meal? Think about sugar content. Mood swings the next day. Whose fault was it they could have something sugary in the first place for that mood swing to happen? Are your kids having the best of a nutritious treat? What are you going to add into your weekly fresh food meal plan for exactly this strategy? Browse online, there many hacks parents are doing for a dessert-like menu. Frozen homemade ice-lollies made from natural fruit juices maybe?

➡ The reason it's best that you create your menu weekly rather than monthly, is so that if you have left-overs from the week before, you can use last week's food before it goes off. You will be able to manage your cash flow better and for your 4th week in the month, plan accordingly with your freezer and left-over food in the fridge. This can bring costs down immensely. Weekly planning is crucial when you have children. Sometimes their timetables and playdates will not always fit into your weekly meal plans, be strategic and buy in perfect quantity for each meal.

SET MEAL PLANNING

SAVING MONEY & TIME
PART 4

BIG TIPS

➡ Plan for the season. Seasonal foods are there to experiment with the kids, as well as making left over meats and vegetables into delicious soups during the winter months. Raw vegetables i.e. chopped tomatoes and carrots are great with houmous during the summer, along with cold meats. Seasonal meal planning is key.

➡ Keep a file for all the kids favourite printed out recipes. List them every week with big, 'got the green light ticks', which you know the kids love to eat and work as family meals. You can create a journal or just use a hardcover pad for this.

➡ Keep a separate file for any up and coming recipes you still want to experiment with. As they get older their tastes change and you can start testing them out on more advanced tasting stews, etc.

➡ Any menus they were not keen on before, put them away in a 'maybe try again later file' for when they are older.

➡ Create an online calendar, which reminds you each week to do your list. Or just do it the good old-fashioned way on a pad stuck to the fridge. Set your alarm on your phone each week as a reminder.

➡ Choose your important shopping day, with little distractions.

➡ Be savvy! Check the sales and don't get caught up in the two-for-one deals unless it's for the month-long dry goods order. Fresh food offers often just go to waste.

- Leftover food planning is key, less waste, more money saving.

- Choose a theme night, Italian, Indian etc.

- Enjoy looking for recipes each week.

- Plan this with your kids. Start getting your eldest involved to mentally prepare them. Show them how to learn from your own strategically well planned-out talents. Involve the kids where you can. Be fair, depending on age - each of them can choose a meal for each night of the week. Fair is fair. And don't forget about you. Choose things that you love too or say it's for you and experiment with something new. Kids often LOVE to eat what mum and dad love to eat!

- Preparation is KEY. (PRIOR PREPARATION PREVENTS POOR PERFORMANCE). Make food from fresh and store in the freezer in batches, well measured out if you must. Use up freezer food monthly.

- Create a group chat with the other mums for winning recipes, tread cautiously for foods where there are allergies. Always ask other parents if their kids have any food allergies during a playdate. Also, what meals suit your meal plan during the week. Will your kid's friends enjoy what you planned?

- Lastly – keep it simple!

YOUR KIDS

HEALTHY MIND, BODY & SOUL

➡ As we all know, or most of us do, without a healthy body there is no healthy mind. And without a healthy brain, mentally this will affect your general well-being, which is our soul. This does not just refer to us as adults. This especially refers to children growing up from babies. What you feed your children will affect their minds as well as their daily routine and bodies. No child, nor adult will function to their maximum potential without a healthy brain, which leads to the functioning of doing small tasks in and around the house and finding it all just a massive painful chore. It can lead to not being able to stick to schedules and managing to physically function with them.

➡ Without your health fully protected and functioning to its full potential, life will drag you down and all the 'springs attached to your machine' will wear away and detach themselves from your motor (your brain). Imagine as a child not being fed well with good nutrients (the springs are not fitting well to the motor, which is the brain function). Is the machine link to the functioning of the springs not firing up because the strength is weak? Well, that is exactly how our bodies work from birth until old age. It does not stop. And in order to keep our machines well oiled, springs not wearing out and our cylinders functioning together 'all in unison', is the only way we will stay alive for a longer period of time. Once we have a few parts of the machinery malfunction, the machine will start to break down slowly and eventually 'the heart of the machine', your brain, will stop completely. If one part of you is not well, the rest starts to pull you down.

➡ That is why MIND, BODY AND SOUL are together as one. Without those three important parts of your machinery, your body will not work to maximum effect. Health comes first, before anything in your life. Even your loved ones. For without health, how are you supposed to support your loved ones? You could have all the money in the world, but without health how are you supposed to enjoy your cash flow? You could be given a great prize for your achievements in life, but if you are unhealthy and not that bothered, how are you supposed to enjoy that praise and achievement if you are not going to live for much longer? Do you see where I'm going with this? Health first, before anything, before anyone.

➡ As parents, you are your first priority with your own health. Why? Because without you and your health in check, how are you supposed to keep your kids' health in check? There is 'a domino' effect here, and it's real and it needs to be taken care of immediately. Our kids did not ask to be born into this world with a certain meal plan in place for their arrival, or exercise plan at birth. This is up to parents to plan before our kids are even born, to make certain they are nurtured as well as taught how to look after themselves from an early age. Parents need to gain knowledge on health, exercise, and nutrition. Health comes first. Without it, we are just disconnected beings on this planet trying out the pieces of our puzzles together, not fully knowing how, or functioning well in the process. By then it might be too late, which it so often is. So come on parents, let us all come together and give the world of support to each other, it will take a team of us to do this. Done right, we are unstoppable.

➡ Wishing you all excellent health, which you will focus on day by day, step by step, starting with you. Be the best parents and teachers you can be. Let us all encourage each other to grow – life is about living to our maximum potential, through mind, body, and soul. Our children, your children, are the future of our tomorrow, so let us prepare them for what is to come and give them the best foundation possible for easier transitioning into a wide open and positive future.

➡ KEEP CALM AND CARRY ON!